Horse Happy

A Complete Guide to Owning Your First Horse

by

Barbara J. Berry

With photographs by James Dandelski
and line illustrations by Terry Nell Morris

The Bobbs-Merrill Company, Inc.
Indianapolis/New York

Published by The Bobbs-Merrill Company, Inc.
Indianapolis   New York

Manufactured in the United States of America
First printing

Library of Congress Cataloging in Publication Data

Berry, Barbara J
  Horse happy.

    Bibliography: p.
    Includes index.
    SUMMARY: A beginner's guide to horse care, with information on stables, tack and equipment, veterinarians, farriers, routines for daily chores, and pointers on riding and training.
    1. Horses—Juvenile literature. [1. Horses]
I. Title.
SF302.B49   636.1   78-55671
ISBN 0-672-52521-6 cloth
ISBN 0-672-52535-6 paper

Horse Happy

Other books by Barbara J. Berry

His Majesty's Mark
The Thoroughbreds
A Look of Eagles
Let 'Er Buck! The Rodeo
Just Don't Bug Me
Shannon

To Frank Hyde, sports editor of the Jamestown, New York, *Post-Journal,* who persuaded me to write the newspaper column that subsequently inspired *Horse Happy*

Acknowledgments

Taking photographs of horses in the midst of a very cold winter presents a multitude of obstacles. But it was made possible, and even enjoyable, by Jim Dandelski, who took most of the pictures and printed them; by Jane Holliday, Buddy Johnson and Mrs. Joe Clark, who provided their barns to take pictures in, and horses to take pictures of; and by the "crews"—Don, Donna, Frankie, Jamie, the two Janes, John, Matt, Sally, Susie and Vera—who shod horses, trimmed winter whiskers, jumped up and down and whistled to get those ears up, and generally proved to be indispensable to the project.

And no acknowledgment would be complete without special mention of the charming cover photo of Katie's Genius. I first came across it in *Saddle & Bridle* magazine (St. Louis, Missouri) as their "Picture Perfect" selection for December 1976, and it was love at first sight. This American Saddlebred gelding now graces our cover, thanks to the kindness and generosity of his owner, Mary Lou Sibley, who also took the picture. Katie's Genius is nineteen years old, has been shown continually since he was two, and is still winning—both fine harness classes, and hearts!

Contents

From Me to You

This book is written for you, the boy or girl who truly loves horses, in the sincere hope that one day soon you will own one. It's a very personal kind of book, written straight from the heart. I know how you feel, because I felt the same way when I was your age. I wanted a horse of my own more than anything else in the world. It was the *only* thing I wanted.

But I learned early that it was out of the question. Although we lived in the country, the aunt and uncle who took me in when I became an orphan at three didn't own the farm we lived on; my uncle was only the manager. So there was all that room—those big barns and all that pastureland—but still "no chance." It was all rather hard for me to understand at the time, and it hurt very much not to be able to have a horse of my own.

But it wasn't a completely horseless existence. Fortunately, although we had tractors to do most of the work, there were also two teams on the farm. The bays were too young and frisky for me, but I begged rides on the big black horses, Prince and Bess, when they came trudging home from their work at dusk. I can still smell the pungent combination of horse sweat and hot dust and feel the harness buckles pinching my legs as I sat high atop blind Prince, clutching the brass hames tightly. I would sit on the wooden hay mangers by the hour, watching those gentle old horses as they ate their well-earned dinners or just napped on their feet. Sometimes, when nobody was looking, I'd climb over from the edge of the manger onto Bess's broad velvety back, just for the pure joy of sitting on a horse. I drew countless "portraits" of their wise, kindly faces. I filled scrapbooks with every horse picture that crossed my path. I dreamed about horses. I pretended I *was* a horse.

Later on, when I was nine, we moved to another farm. Here too I was lucky, in that there was still a team of horses, a pair of beautiful red roan Belgian mares. The younger one, Daisy, was too cranky to play with, but Kate was my love. She was sixteen or seventeen, and silvery colored. She was very tall and as round as a barrel, but somehow I'd manage to drag boxes into her stall, pile them up, and climb up to sit on *her* back, too. Eventually my persistence prevailed, and I won permission to ride her. With endless patience she carried me around the farm at a slow plod—with maybe a little trot now and then. Our tack consisted entirely of a blinkered work bridle with a piece of clothesline tied to the bit for reins. For a riding habit I usually wore a shirt, shorts and sneakers. All summer I had sticky legs—from horse sweat. In the winter I wore all the warm clothing I owned. This was my grand beginning as a horseman.

Since then I've ridden some pretty nice horses, including five-gaited Saddlebreds, and I've even owned a horse or two. I've had a lot of enjoyment from it all. But no horse can ever be to me what old Kate was when I was ten or twelve years old, because I can never again feel about a horse the way I felt when I was that age—your age. They say there's a best time for everything, and I think the best time to get your own horse is when that horse is the most important thing in the world to you.

Some of you who are reading this book will soon be getting a horse of your own. I hope you'll find my advice helpful. But I know that for lots of you it may be a long wait, as it was for me. If that is the case, you may be the luckiest ones, after all. Your horse, for the time being, will be imaginary, and in some ways that's the best kind. You can have whatever kind of horse strikes your fancy—a different one every day, if you want—with no chores and no problems, ever!

And—please try to believe me when I tell you this—planning for a horse, looking forward to it, is at least half the fun! Not only that, but the longer you must wait—the more time you have to plan and prepare—the more successful your first venture is likely to be.

So while this is for you who are about to embark on your first experience as a horse owner, it's just as much for you who will be waiting awhile longer. It's for all of us, really, who are afflicted with that wonderfully incurable condition known as being horse happy.

Chapter One:
What to Do
Until the Horse Arrives

The first thing to do to get ready for future horse ownership, whenever it may be, is go to the library and the bookstore, stock up on horse books, hole up somewhere, and read. You've probably been doing this for years, but now you have a purpose—to learn and remember. There are lots of horse magazines out these days, too, with a variety of interesting and helpful articles. Read all of them you can find.

To begin with, try to keep your mind open about what kinds of horses to learn about. I think it's a shame that most horse people decide on a favorite breed and then forevermore wear blinkers in regard to all the other breeds. An "Arabian freak" wouldn't give you two cents for a Saddlebred, for instance; while a quarter horse man might not even consider giving stall space to an Arabian. In other words, many horse people let themselves get so partial to one breed or kind of horse that they cut themselves off from the rest of the horse world. What a lot they're missing! And the worst of it is, so many people choose their favorite breed for no good, sensible reason at all—it just happens. Maybe the people up the road have quarter horses or one of their friends just bought a Morgan.

Try hard not to be like that. Give careful thought to selecting a breed while you're "looking around" in books and magazines. It's entirely possible that you'll run across one you've never even considered before and fall madly in love with it. (In all your daydreaming, for instance, have you ever thought of getting a Tennessee Walking Horse?)

But there's something you should consider before you start even to read about the various breeds: people who write a book or an article about a particular breed of horse are sometimes very biased. So it's wise to be just a little suspicious about all the wonderful qualities you'll be told about, and to try to find out about some of the less attractive traits. Beyond that, keep in mind that while it's all well and good to talk about breed traits—and they certainly exist—what's more important is each individual horse and its own individual traits. A breed might be noted

1

far and wide for its docility, for instance, but that doesn't guarantee that the specimen *you're* thinking about buying hasn't been mistreated into a sour disposition. Breed traits are only a general guideline. And, while we're on the subject of partiality, keep in mind that it goes both ways. Don't pay too much attention to "slurs and aspersions" cast against "other" breeds by biased authors. I've read some pretty wild accusations about Saddlebreds, for example, that I know for pure fact are a lot of balderdash. (Such accusations in regard to Saddlebreds are invariably made by authors who are extremely knowledgeable about hunters and jumpers, but who I suspect have never been closer than fifty yards to a Saddlebred!)

When you've read everything you can get your hands on about every breed possible, then it's time to go talk with horse people. Again, don't talk only with people who raise a particular breed. Seek out folks who have to deal with all kinds of horses. Veterinarians usually have some sound opinions, and farriers—blacksmiths who shoe horses—often have some very firm ones! And if you can find professional horse

You should take full advantage of the tremendous amount of material available to the new or prospective horse owner. Raid the library, find a quiet corner, bring a quiet friend, and **read. (Photo by John Dandelski.)**

trainers who have had experience with several different breeds, they can be an excellent source of inside information.

Even then, you're going to find a great deal of contradiction. This is part and parcel of the horse business. There may just possibly be one or two things that all horsemen agree on, but I'd be hard put to think what they are! So one trainer you talk with might say he won't touch Appaloosas because "they're so dumb," while the next trainer may just love to work with them. Horse trainers, in fact, can be the most prejudiced of all horse people, depending on their experiences. But when you have talked with enough of them, and with enough vets and farriers, and allowed for the occasional grain of salt, you will begin to get a fairly accurate picture.

And don't forget the people who own and work in boarding stables, where they get all kinds. If there is anyone who knows something about horses' temperaments, it's the person who has to work around them every day. Again, try to talk with enough of these people to get an all-around picture. I keep saying this because very often a horseman will have an aversion to a whole breed just because of one or two bad experiences. This is understandable—you have to allow for his being human, too. Just see what somebody else has to say about a breed, and then somebody else, before you make up your own mind.

Another thing you should be doing while you're reading and talking with people about horses is learning how to ride them. And it's even more important to begin to learn how to handle them. You'll be spending a lot more time working around and with your horse than you'll be spending on its back. Right now, for example, can you longe a horse without getting tangled up in the line? Do you stagger around with dizziness after two or three circles? Do you know the correct way to lead a horse through a narrow doorway, and the safe way to let go of it after you've led it into its stall? In other words, can you take good care of a horse by yourself, without putting yourself continually in danger?

It's possible, I suppose, to wait till you get the horse to learn all these things. But surely that's the hard way. (And it's also possible that neither you nor the horse will make it through the first week, using that method.) So you really should make an effort to find a good barn somewhere nearby where you can learn by watching and doing. You need a good place to "hang around." This means, first of all, a place you can get to regularly. Maybe you'll be lucky and just have to walk down the road a piece; maybe one of your parents or an older brother or sister will take you; maybe a bus will drop you off close enough. If it's at all possible, do get some firsthand experience.

Be careful, though. No barn at all is better than a bad one. I can show you what I mean by a good barn just by telling you a little bit about the one where I hang out a lot. If you find one like it, don't hesitate to become a regular.

This barn is clean. The stalls are "done" thoroughly on a regular basis, come what may. They're always kept deeply bedded with clean, dry sawdust. They are roomy and sturdily built; there are no protruding nails to cause injury. The barn itself is well lit and well ventilated and is warm in winter. (Well, relatively warm—here in western New York *no* barn is really "warm" in winter!) The tack room is crowded, but it's neat enough so that things can be found when they're needed, and the tack is clean.

The wide center aisle between the rows of box stalls is covered with a nonslip rubber mat. Each stall has its own cross-tie rings and an overhead light. The horses are fed and watered and exercised on a strict schedule, and they are *well* fed, watered and exercised. There are no "ribby" horses in this barn. And—something for you to watch for—the place is always busy. You can tell a lot from that, because a busy barn is a well-run barn where things get done.

Most important of all, though: the people at the barn are great.

(LEFT) Get some real experience with horses before you bring one home to live with you. It always helps to make friends with someone who already has a horse and will share it with you. (Photo by Lois Rappaport, courtesy of the American Saddle Horse Breeders Association.) *(RIGHT) At your learning barn you'll find out how to handle horses from the ground, too—even cantankerous ones that "talk back," like Archie. Matt eventually won this debate, by the way.* (Photo by James Dandelski, courtesy of Holliday Farm.)

They're willing to answer endless questions—if you're willing to follow them around while they work. They're willing to let a beginner learn by doing, even though that means they'll have to supervise jobs they could probably do better and faster themselves. This is essential for your purposes. The biggest, cleanest, best-run barn in the world won't help you much if the people who run it aren't the sort to take time to teach a youngster.

At my barn the woman who owns it also gives riding instruction, and this is what you should try for. Once or twice a week you can take your lessons, and in between you can learn how to handle a horse from the ground. But maybe you'll find one barn where there is no teacher but where the folks are congenial and helpful, and another barn where the opposite is true. Go to both if you can, of course. But if you have to make a choice, I'd advise you to go to the barn run by the nice people. You'll have more fun and you'll learn more.

Moreover, once you've become good friends, these people will surely help you choose your first horse. In that case, you'll be likely to get a good one that will be safe for you to learn to ride by yourself. Riding, in short, comes second to learning how to handle horses safely. Not only that, but while you're helping your new friends clean stalls and lug water buckets, you'll be building up some muscles and callouses—items you'll be very glad you have, when your own horse arrives. Taking good care of a horse demands quite a lot of strength and stamina.

All right, now, where do we stand? You're reading a lot; you're

A good riding instructor will show you what all the books mean. Here Jane Holliday instructs Matt, while Archie waits more or less patiently. (Photo by James Dandelski, courtesy of Holliday Farm.)

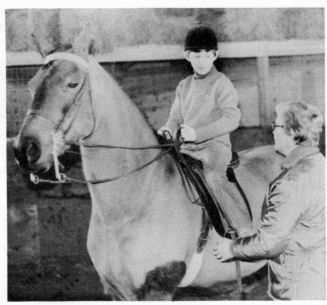

questioning everybody who'll hold still long enough; you're going to a barn as often as you can manage it; and maybe you're getting some riding lessons, too. Now why don't you see if you can get into a good horse club? Horse ownership isn't always required, and even if it is, you can at least investigate the local clubs beforehand. If your county has an active 4-H Club horse program, by all means get involved. Many communities also have saddle clubs, but such clubs can vary widely as to quality. Some might be good for you to join and some might not. That's why I think you should find out what they're like before you jump in with both front feet. At any rate, a riding club with your kind of people who ride the way you like to ride can add considerably to your enjoyment, especially if it sponsors little horse shows.

Which brings us to yet another useful project that will add to your growing supply of horse sense. Go to as many horse shows as you can: the bigger the better, and especially the big, all-breed shows. There you'll get a good opportunity to see all the varieties of horses. Watch every single class—western pleasure, English pleasure, park classes, Morgan, Arabian, and Saddlebred. One thing you'll see right away is that a particular breed of horse can often be used and shown in several different ways. As an example, a Saddlebred horse might be a pleasure horse, a three-gaited horse, a five-gaited horse, a fine harness horse, or a pleasure driving horse. This alone may be an eye opener to you. On top of that, you will learn at a big horse show that a "pleasure horse" can be English, western, Arabian, Morgan, Saddlebred, et cetera. In other words, there's a great big wide-open choice out there. All the more reason to watch it all, read it all, talk with everybody, and take your time about making up your mind.

And now we get to what may be the most difficult part—talking it over with the rest of the family. Your parents and brothers and sisters should know ahead of time what to expect, too, from what amounts to a new member of the family. Maybe everybody is in favor of the idea, but do they all realize that if you get sick some blustery winter day, one of them may have to "do chores," and do they know what that means? How do they feel about it? Do they love horses as much as you do, or does the very thought strike terror?

Do your parents realize that a horse needs re-shoeing—or at least trimming and resetting—every six or eight weeks, and do they know what that costs? Your parents, after all, have the last say about the horse—whether you can have it at all, whether you can build a barn or will board it out, and so on. In all fairness, they should be given some idea about how much this is going to cost them. And it isn't only a matter of fairness. About the worst thing I can think of—much worse than never getting a horse at all—would be to get one and then have to give it up later because nobody had fully realized how fast and how high all those little bills add up! Anyway, let's face it—if you haven't made it all clear, everybody is going to find out soon enough.

But why should your parents have to foot all the bills? No one expects a schoolkid to earn enough money to buy a horse, build a barn, and support the whole thing by himself. However, you should be eager to help all you possibly can. What can you do to earn money in the time left after school and homework—and horse chores? Babysit? Do yard work? Shovel snow? It depends, of course, on where you live and what opportunities are open to you. So talk it all out. If you're willing and able to make a contribution, however much of a drop in the bucket it may be, maybe your parents will be more agreeable to the idea.

At least you will have made it clear to them that you understand some of the realities of the situation, from an economic standpoint. You might also make it clear that you understand a few other realities: that a horse is more than just an expensive toy; that it's a living, breathing, manure-pile-building creature that will demand hours of work every week. I know you think you'll love every minute of it, but the fact remains that that animal will be out there in that barn every single morning and night waiting to be attended to, whether it's a lovely spring day or whether it's twenty below zero and a blizzard is raging and the snow has piled up in front of the barn door again and the bucket is solid with ice and everything takes twice as long to do because your fingers are so cold and you think you're going to *die. Nobody* loves that, and you won't, either!

But if you can convince your parents that you know all this, and that you realize that owning a horse is not going to be one continual gallop through a field of flowers, it might help you and your cause.

So get busy. Read. Go to a barn and work and learn. Talk with all kinds of horse people. Go to horse shows. And figure out a way to earn some money. If you do, sooner or later your dream will come true.

Chapter Two: Basic Horse Talk

Each part of the horse world has its own language—terms and phrases that might mean little to the other segments. People who raise, train and ride Morgan show horses, for example, express themselves in terms rarely used by trainers of hunter-jumpers or racehorses or quarter horses. These different segments, in fact, are almost worlds unto themselves.

But when you get started on the serious business of actually looking at horses and talking to their would-be sellers, you'll want to be able to understand some of the language that's common to all horse-men—"basic horse talk." It's surprisingly simple. You won't really need to know all that much, and you certainly won't have to carry a dictionary around with you to understand what's being said and maybe even to sound somewhat horse-wise yourself.

Let's start with horse families and learn the various words that describe the members of a family with respect to sex, age and relationships.

A horse's mother is called its *dam*. There are two ways to get this idea across; one is to say that Clover Blossom is the dam of Leadfoot; the other, that Leadfoot is *out of* Clover Blossom.

The father of a horse is called its *sire*. Again, we can say that Leadfoot's sire is Old Conestoga, or that Leadfoot is *by* Old Conestoga. Leadfoot, then, would be said to be "by Old Conestoga out of Clover Blossom."

Leadfoot, being male, was a *colt* until he was four or five years old. Some people consider a horse grown up at four and some at five. Technically, colts are always males, but in different parts of the country—or parts of the horse world—you might hear the terms horse colt and mare colt. They may not be strictly correct, but they're certainly clear enough.

A *filly* is what people mean when they say "mare colt." A female horse is a filly until she is four or five years old.

All baby horses are *foals* until they're weaned, when they become

8

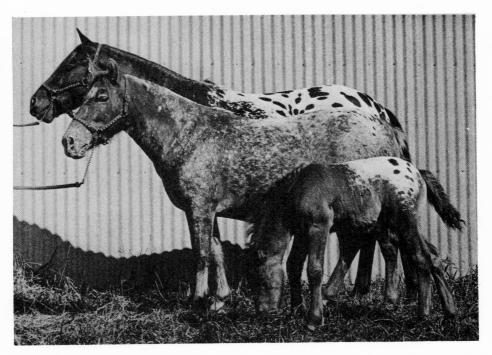

An unusual photo that illustrates three of our definitions in one: sire *(REAR),* dam *and* foal. *The little Pony of the Americas foal seems to be a compromise between his sire's loud coloring and his dam's more subtle markings.* (Photo courtesy of Mrs. John Delahoy.)

weanlings. On their first birthday they graduate to becoming *yearlings.* Again, you may hear someone say "colt foal" or "filly foal," which is just more descriptive—it tells you not only the approximate age but also the sex.

A *mare* is a full-grown female horse.

A *stallion* is a grown male horse that is "entire," or not castrated, and is therefore able to sire foals.

A *stud* isn't quite the same thing as a stallion, in that rightfully a stallion should only be called a stud if he's actually used for breeding. A place where horses are bred and raised is also called a stud.

Colts are usually castrated when they aren't going to be used for breeding. This is a surgical procedure in which the testicles are removed. Since the surgery also removes all or nearly all sexual notions at the same time, the resulting horse, called a *gelding,* is usually easier to get along with. He doesn't have all those distractions to contend with, and neither do you. This isn't to say that stallions are necessarily difficult animals. Many of them are very quiet and have lovely dispositions. And it certainly isn't to say that all geldings are perfect. But, generally speaking, according to most horsemen, a given horse is more reliably even tempered and will give you fewer problems after gelding than will the same horse ungelded. In any case, few horsemen recommend that a youngster buy a stallion for a riding horse and backyard pet.

Once a horse gets through the foal and filly or colt phases, it's described age-wise about the same as you are. If it's twelve years old, it's a twelve-year-old. Most registered horses have a birthday on January 1, however, regardless of when they were really foaled, which gives rise to such odd-sounding terms as *long yearling* (one born early in the year) and *short yearling* (one unfortunate enough to have arrived later). A horse that's just over three and a half years old might be called a coming four-year-old. And an unregistered horse past nine is an *aged* horse. So is a registered one, but when a horse is registered, there's no question about precisely how old it is. With an unregistered horse, a great deal is sometimes left to the seller's discretion—and imagination.

Until a horse is about nine years old, any knowledgeable person can tell its age just by peering at its teeth, but after that it goes from uncertain to impossible. I found, when I was looking around at horses, that there are a surprising number of nine-year-olds on the market! In fact I bought one on approval, and as soon as I got her home I called my vet, who said she was probably fifteen. So I'd be inclined, if I were you, to interpret "nine" with no registration certificate as meaning at *least* nine and have it checked out first thing.

Another point sometimes open to interpretation is whether you're looking at a pony or a horse. If you're not going to be showing the

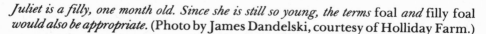

Juliet is a filly, one month old. Since she is still so young, the terms foal *and* filly foal *would also be appropriate.* (Photo by James Dandelski, courtesy of Holliday Farm.)

animal, it doesn't make any difference, as long as it's of a size to suit you. But since horse-show classes sometimes require a very accurate definition, and measurement to the inch, it might pay you to know.

A pony is anything up to and including 14.2 hands, while a horse is anything over that. A hand is four inches, and the number after the decimal point does not mean two-tenths of a hand—it means two inches! Deciphered, then—if you're still with me—14.2 hands means fourteen hands plus two inches, or fifty-eight inches. (And ponies are often measured in straight inches rather than hands; for example, a "fifty-six-inch pony.")

In terms of horse shows, this whole thing can be exasperating. There are a lot of equines that stand about 14.2 hands. Are they horses or ponies? You have to measure at the highest point of the withers. Then there are the smaller breeds, like Arabians, that are definitely considered horses, but some of them, being under 14.2 hands, are technically ponies. And *then* there are the Saddlebreds! Here confusion can not only reign but positively run amok. Both five-gaited and three-gaited Saddlebreds have classes for "under-twos," which are horses 15.2 and under, and for "over-twos," anything *over* 15.2 hands. (Not to mention classes for Saddlebred ponies.) You can wear out a measuring stick in a Saddle Horse barn. My first horse, Mark, was an under-two when his hooves were trimmed down short, but an over–two with long hooves and pads.

Then, having gotten all this straightened out, you'll be faced with yet another possible source of confusion. There are three words that are still often misused, although things are improving along those lines. The first one is *purebred*. A purebred horse is one all of whose ancestors on both sides are of the same breed. The second word is *thoroughbred,* which some people still think means the same as purebred. It doesn't. A Thoroughbred (usually capitalized) is a specimen of a distinct breed of horse, bred for speed at the gallop. So if someone tells you that he owns a "thoroughbred Arabian," he could be telling you that his horse is a cross between a Thoroughbred and an Arabian (in which case it's an "Anglo-Arab" and can be registered as such), or he could be telling you that he's confusing his terms and what he really has is a *purebred* Arabian. A professional horseman won't mix you up like this, but the casual horse owner might.

The third word is *registered*. All this means is that a horse has been registered with a recognized breed registry, or perhaps with one of the color registries, or with one of the halfbreed registries. If you buy a registered horse, be very sure that you get the certificate, all up to date and easily transferable to your name. All horses registered with breed registries are purebreds; some registered with color or other registries are purebred; and not all purebreds are registered. And a purebred Thoroughbred is eligible for registration.

Now let's get around to horse colors. You can have a lot of fun figuring out some of these, as horsemen have a peculiar way of describing them. Sometimes the different breed people even have different names for the same color, or have fanciful terms for them, just as dog breeders do with their fawn and brindle and blue merle and so on. (I like my dog's—he's a Chesapeake Bay retriever, and his color is described rather starkly as "brown.")

But what is liver chestnut to a Saddlebred or Morgan person might be seal-brown, dark bay or (like my dog) plain brown to a Standardbred man. And while a horse may look black to you or me, if he has even a few brown hairs around the edges, technically he's not black but bay or brown or liver chestnut or something else.

Generally speaking, though, "bay" is a reddish-brown color, ranging from quite light to very dark, with a black mane and tail, and usually black lower legs ("black points") as well. Often a particularly red shade of bay is referred to as blood bay, and a very rich, dark one as mahogany bay. A chestnut horse might have the same body color as a bay, but if its mane and tail are the same shade as or lighter than its body, then it's chestnut instead. Western people seem to prefer the word sorrel for this color combination. Chestnuts, or sorrels, never have black legs, but both bays and chestnuts often have white markings on their legs. "Stockings" are usually up to the knees and hocks, and "socks" are about halfway up or less.

Just about any color horse can have white markings on its face, too. A small white patch on the forehead is called a star; a wide white strip down the center of the face is a blaze; a narrow one is a stripe; and if a horse has a blaze that widens to include its eyes and/or its muzzle, it is said to be bald faced.

Bay, chestnut and brown are by far the colors most often seen. Another common one is gray, which can be nearly black or nearly white. Often a gray horse will change from one to the other during its lifetime, starting out as a foal almost black and aging into a nearly white old horse. Some grays, however, are born almost black and never lighten up very much, remaining steel-gray for the bulk of their lives.

Liver chestnut is an unattractive term for a beautiful color—a chocolate brown. A liver chestnut with a pale, flaxen mane and tail is a striking animal.

Roans can be either red roan or blue roan. In the former case, white hairs are interspersed almost equally with bay hairs; in the other, with black or very dark hairs. Roans are more common in some breeds than others, being rare among Saddlebreds, for instance, but very often seen in Tennessee Walkers.

Palomino is a gold color complemented with a white mane and tail. Some pure breeds do have this color among their ranks, but quite often a palomino is of mixed blood. Buckskin is another color rarely seen in many of our riding horse breeds, but often in others, such as quarter horses. It too is "golden," but the range of shading is wide, from almost creamy to almost bay. There are horses that might be called either light

Apple Cash was the first American Buckskin Registry Association champion, and one of the foundation sires of ABRA. Note the black legs, mane and tail, and the distinct dorsal stripe. (Photo courtesy of the American Buckskin Registry Association.)

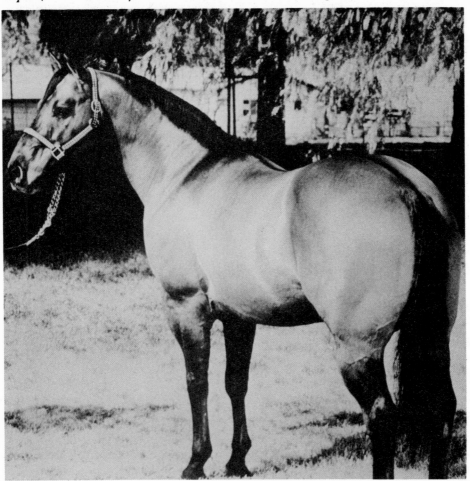

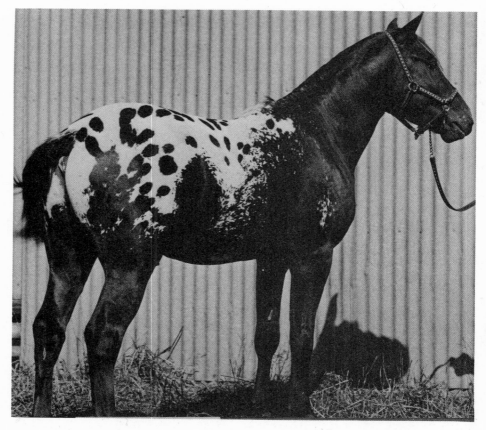

Jack Spots is a P.O.A. stallion, with the greatly desired flashy coloring and round, powerful conformation of that breed. P.O.A.s, being medium-sized ponies, make wonderful horses for children. (Photo courtesy of Mrs. John Delahoy.)

bay or buckskin, except that buckskin horses have a dark stripe, called a dorsal stripe, along their spines. They also have black or very dark manes and tails, whereas the palomino's are white. There is a registry for buckskins, too.

Spotted horses can also be registered. Some are purebreds, and some are registered primarily on the basis of coloring. Called pintos or paints (or just plain "spotted horses"), they have bay or black in some areas of their bodies and pure white in others. Appaloosas, another kind of "spotted horse," are registered mostly on pedigree and are purebred, but coloring plays a large part in that breed, and the color has to be right for registration. Some Appies are black or red on white; others are white on red or black; and there are many markings that are unique to the breed, such as white "blankets" over the rumps, and sprinklings of white that look like spilled sugar. This is probably the most colorful breed of all. In fact, Appaloosa fanciers will brag about a "loud-colored" one.

You could spend a whole week looking at Appaloosas and never see two that looked the same. A smaller version of the Appaloosa, the P.O.A. (Pony of the Americas) is marked just as flashily.

Sometimes the color of a horse depends on the time of the year you're looking at it. I've noticed several whose summer coats differed noticeably in color from their winter coats. Grays' often do, and Mark, who was liver chestnut in the summer when I bought him, startled me by turning bright red for the winter: the only horse I'd known with "red winter woollies."

Now, let's say you've been looking and listening awhile, and you know enough to remark very casually, "Oh, say, isn't that a handsome little bay under-two filly?" What if the owner asks you if you want him to "park her out" for you? Well, that's simple—just say, "Yes, please," and you'll soon find out that he's talking about asking the horse to "come up on her feet." He'll make sure the horse is standing with her back legs straight and even, and then ask her to come forward with just the front feet, so that the body is somewhat "stretched" (another word that means the same as parking out) and she's looking her very best. Head up, ears alert . . . it's picture-taking time. If possible, you'll want your horse to have been trained to do this, by the way, and not just for taking pictures. It's a terrific way to get an eager-beaver horse to stand still while you mount.

With a horse parked out, it's time to talk conformation. For instance, is he fine or coarse? If he's fine, he has small bones, slender legs and

If your horse won't stand still for you to mount, train him to park out, like Bandero here. Once he's learned that, you shouldn't have any problem. Besides, some breeds are required to park out in the show ring, for the judge's examination. (Photo by James Dandelski, courtesy of Buddy Johnson Stables.)

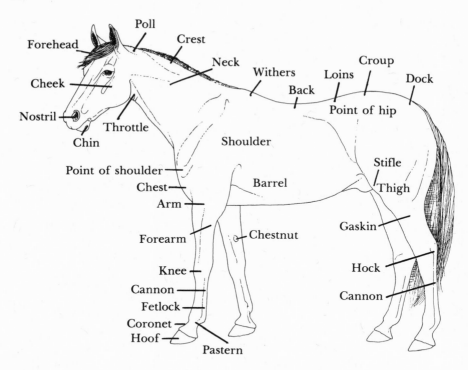

neck, and a neat, delicate-looking head. This is more important in some breeds than in others. People looking for a heavy hunter wouldn't be interested in a horse that's "fine as a deer." But no horse should be really coarse, to the point where you wonder if his daddy was a draft horse.

Listen closely to everything the seller says, especially if he's an old-time dealer-trainer. These people are wonderful, and you'll pick up some fascinating horse talk from them. They usually have a very colorful way of expressing themselves. A long-barreled horse, for instance, "stands over a lot of ground," while a tall one is "well up on legs." (This is not to be confused with being "well legged up," which means the legs are strongly muscled.) And I once heard an old-timer reminiscing about a horse he'd bought in a weak moment that turned out to have what might most kindly have been described as a breathing problem. *"Talk?"* he said. "Why, that horse talked like a radio, and when he got warmed up good, he sounded like a pig with its head stuck in the gate. He could really whistle you a tune!" So, listen! You may be entertained as well as educated.

And remember, don't ever ask how tall a horse is. You want to know "how high he stands." And beware of descriptions like "spirited." For one thing, I've never in my life heard a real horseman use that word, so it might be a clue that the fellow isn't one. For another, "spirited" might be exactly what you don't want, even if you think you do. It may mean happy, cheerful, good-natured and willing, or it may mean the horse is ornery as a bedbug and twice as hard to control.

On the other hand, if you're assured that the horse is "real quiet," he could turn out to be like another horse I brought home once for a ten-day-free-trial period, a grossly overweight cream-colored gelding we called Fat Albert for the short time we kept him. Real quiet? He was practically catatonic. The only time I ever saw him put on any speed at all was when I brought his grain to him. He'd whip across the stall for that, but otherwise—*real* quiet! Sometimes I wondered if I shouldn't hold a mirror to his nostrils, just to be sure.

The most important word for you to keep an ear out for, though, is "sound." "Guaranteed sound" is even better. It means healthy—free of diseases and ailments, and of weaknesses that might easily cause diseases and ailments. Maybe you've heard the expression "sound in wind and limb." This is what your horse should be. And don't forget the "wind" part. A horse that has to work like crazy just to breathe isn't going to be of much use to you. One that's afflicted with emphysema, a common ailment among older horses, for instance, is usually referred to as being "a little heavey." If you hear that, seriously consider saying thank you and good-by. We can leave most of this end of it to your vet, but by listening you may save him a trip. *If* you know what you're hearing.

When you set out to talk to horsemen, you should also be acquainted with the terms for the various gaits and know exactly what they mean. Most horses will walk, trot and canter, just doing what comes naturally. (One exception that springs instantly to mind is the Tennessee Walking Horse, which isn't supposed to trot, ever, but sometimes does, very nicely.)

The walk is easy—everyone has seen a horse walk. But next time you do, really pay attention. You'll see that it's a slow, four-beat (one foot at a time) gait, head nodding, with a gentle up-and-down motion to the back. You've surely seen horses trot, too. This is faster, of course, as the horse puts more "push" into it, and this time it's a two-beat gait, because the horse touches ground with two feet at the same time. *(Listen* to it, on a hard surface.) And since they're the two feet on opposite corners, the trot is also called a diagonal gait. At the trot, the back rises and falls much more noticeably than at the walk because of the extra propulsion from the hindquarters. A jog is a nice, slow, easy trot.

The canter is a three-beat gait (listen!), meaning that two of the feet touch ground at the same time, while the other two touch at intervals. The horse always "leads" on one side or the other at the canter, and he's said to be on his right lead or on his left lead, the leading leg reaching out first and farther than the other one, both fore and aft. He's "on the wrong lead" when he doesn't take the one you asked him for or, if he's loose, when he goes around a circle leading on the outside legs, something a horse will rarely do. Cross-cantering is another thing altogether, and it means the horse is leading on one side in front and on the other side behind. It's difficult to describe, but if your horse cross-canters you'll feel it right away. You might not know what he's doing, but you'll realize that it's something strange.

People who ride stock seat (more about that later) don't canter their horses; they "lope" them. It isn't entirely a difference in terminology. A canter is different technically from a lope, too, in that a canter by definition is really a "collected gait" in which the horse is to some degree "bringing his length together" between your hands (restraining him) and your legs (pushing him on). Therefore a cantering horse's head will be higher and his knees and hocks will achieve more elevation than those of a horse that's loping, uncollected, on a loose rein. Horses in pasture may either lope or canter, depending on their breeding and how they are feeling at the moment. A horse that's "feelin' good" will collect *himself*.

As Denmark's Day Dream trots along, you can readily see how the legs on opposite corners work in unison. Compare this with the next photo of a horse racking. (Photo by Sargent, courtesy of the American Saddle Horse Breeders Association.)

Mountjoy's American Aristocrat, a Saddlebred five-gaited gelding ridden by Jane Roitenberg, demonstrates the rack. Note the high action. At this instant, only the near forehoof is actually touching the ground; when the stride has been completed, all four hooves will have touched, one at a time, creating the four-beat gait. (Photo by Holvoet, courtesy of Keith D. Bartz, Hollow Haven Farm, Chanhassen, Minnesota, president of the United Professional Horsemen's Association.)

The gallop, which almost any horse performs naturally, is executed in the same way as a canter or a lope, but it's faster than either and is less collected than a canter. A horse that's galloping rather slowly and well in hand is said to be doing a hand gallop, while a horse that's galloping really fast is said to be running.

Some horses pace naturally, too. This is about the same speed as a trot, but the legs on *each side* move together, instead of the "opposite corners" moving together, so it's called a lateral gait. This "sidewheeling" leg movement makes the back sway from side to side rather than go up and down, and depending on how smoothly the horse paces, it can be quite nice to ride, or rather horrible. Obviously the rider can't post, or "rise," as he can at the trot, so if the gait is rough you just have to sit there and take it. If you buy a Standardbred, you can expect that it's likely to be a pacer, since most Standardbreds are these days.

Many horses also single-foot naturally, since most of our light horse breeds have single-footing—and/or pacing—ancestors. The term itself is very descriptive since in this gait a single foot touches the ground at a time. That makes it a four-beat gait, like the walk, but the cadence is quicker, and there's a certain amount of "lift" to it. The effect, for the rider, is so smooth it's almost as though the horse were rolling along on casters.

From this single-foot came the "horse show" gaits of the five-gaited

Saddlebred and the running walk of the Tennessee Walker. The Saddlebred's slow-gait and rack are both four-beat gaits and are examples of taking advantage of—and cultivating—a natural tendency. When a Saddlebred show horse slow-gaits and racks, he does it with what is called brilliance. By nature, training, and sometimes shoeing, the five-gaited Saddlebred executes all his gaits in a highly collected fashion, his head high and neck well flexed, his knees and hocks coming up extremely high. And somehow he manages to do the rack—the exciting high-speed gait—at upward of thirty miles an hour, to boot. Pleasure Saddlebreds can often do all these gaits, too, but with less motion, which makes for a very agreeable ride.

The running walk of the Tennessee Walking Horse is another cultivated gait and is perhaps the hardest of all to describe. About the best way I can express it is to say that it "flows." The Walker is expected to do a flat walk, the faster running walk, and a highly collected rolling canter. If you haven't seen anything but the plain walk, trot and canter before, get out to some horse shows; you're going to be astonished.

Now, if you study all this, and practice up on throwing out phrases like "Don't you really think he's a little low in the back?" (a nicer way of saying swaybacked) or "Let him trot on a little and we'll see how square he is," you might be able to pass yourself off as a horseman. More important, you may understand what the real horsemen are trying to tell you. And if you really listen, every visit will add more to your vocabulary, so spend a lot more time listening than talking.

But before you do any actual *buying*, you'll have to figure out an answer to one big question: Where do you *put* a thousand-pound animal?

Chapter Three:
A Roof Over His Head

In most parts of the country, a horse should have some kind of shelter. In some parts, such as here in western New York, he *needs* it. Not that a horse by nature is a delicate, fragile creature—far from it. Some horses can withstand even one of our northern-type winters with little more than a pine tree to stand under when it hails. They simply grow a heavy, shaggy coat and tough it out. But those are horses that aren't interfered with too much by people.

In a natural state, horses don't move around at high speed all that much, especially in the winter. If they did, their lungs might get "burned" from super-cold air rushing in too fast, and they might founder or get pneumonia from working up a sweat under all that winter hair and then cooling off suddenly. So they just mooch around, usually, digging through the snow for their food and generally cooperating with nature in keeping their body temperatures about right.

It's *people* who make shelter necessary for horses, by breeding some of them for fine coats, for instance, or by demanding that they exercise heavily in cold weather, either for recreation or in order to have them well trained and muscled for the spring shows. So the matter of shelter is more or less up to you and how you'll be using your horse. Even if you live where the winters are severe, all you'll really need is a little three-sided shed inside a paddock, if you're willing to allow the horse's coat to grow unattractively shaggy and if you're sure you won't be asking it to exert itself to the sweating point in very cold weather. Most people, however, rebel at the idea of having to support a horse for twelve months just so they can ride it for about six.

So let's assume for the moment that you live where the winters get pretty tough, and where there is room—at least an acre or two—to build a little barn, and where the zoning laws and the neighbors won't prohibit such a structure. Let's also assume that—even better yet—you have some choice as to where to locate the barn on your property.

There's really no point in situating the barn so far from the house that merely getting to it in the winter will be a long-distance endurance test. Or in building it so close that the open kitchen window gets the full benefit of every breeze from that direction. Or in putting it just across the fence from the neighbor's barbecue pit so that the arrival of the horse is very soon followed by a demand for its departure—and its smelly pile with it! Let's face it—horses have a lot of sterling virtues, but being highly sanitary is not one of them. Truly horse-happy people never notice this, but other less enlightened people sometimes do! Unless you live way out in the country with no other houses close by, your neighbors will have to love horses, too, or at least be very tolerant of them. Even so, try not to put the barn right on the boundary line, if you want to remain on good terms with them.

Having found a good spot for a barn, then, between one and two hundred feet from the house and not too near the neighbors, there are a few other things to consider about the location. A horse loves to stand under a tree in the summer. If there is a big shady one in a likely area, by all means take advantage of it. Maybe you can build your paddock around it. And try to avoid building a horse barn in a gully. A barn and paddock should both be on ground high enough for good drainage, if it's at all possible. No matter where it's located, after a couple of good rains your paddock will be a mass of muck for a while—horses have a marvelous way of churning it up—but the better drained it is, the faster it'll dry off.

We usually do our building in the summer, of course. But when you're planning the location of your barn, look ahead to the winter. For example, it seems sensible to put the barn door—the one you'll be using when you do chores—on the side toward the house. But comes the winter, and you may find that this is the *very* place where the snowdrifts pile up. That's what happened to me. We remodeled an old building ourselves, and as it happened, that's where the door was—precisely where the snow piled up. After struggling the five hundred or so feet through a howling blizzard, I had to shovel frantically just to get the door open, while, inside, the lonely, breakfastless horse nearly tore the walls down around his ears trying to get me to hurry up! So take it from me—think winter. If snowdrifts usually pile up on the south side of your house, they'll probably do the same on the barn. Why make your chores that much harder?

Even more important, you'll want to be able to get to the barn in the winter with a truck or a station wagon. You may even need to put in a driveway. It's wise to buy enough hay and bedding to last you all winter, but if your barn is very small, you may not be able to store that much. And how about the farrier? If he can't get his truck to the barn door, he'll have to carry all his equipment, and I don't know a single farrier whose idea of a good time is lugging an anvil and a box full of heavy tools through hip-deep snow or down an icy hill. So make sure the barn will be accessible all year 'round.

Another thing we tend to forget about in the summer is how heavy the snow can get. Those of you who live "up North" had better not build a barn with an absolutely flat roof. Several such roofs actually caved in around here last winter. One was over a brand-new, contractor-built indoor arena, and it collapsed just minutes after a group of people had left it. In the right weather conditions, that snow can easily add up to tons. Of course, you can always shovel the roof, but who needs that, on top of everything else?

A peaked roof is not only prettier but more economical, since it adds storage space relatively inexpensively. A traditional hipped "barn roof" is probably the best of all, because it adds even more space. It's a matter of practicality, really. If you're going to keep your horse at home all year 'round, you'll need supplies for it—hay, bedding, feed. You *can* build a barn with only enough room for the stall and a little areaway in front of it, and then haul in hay, bedding and feed every week or so. A lot of people do this, but frankly it sounds to me like a pain in the neck. Besides, I'm the worrying kind: What if we should get one of our blizzard-a-week winters and I couldn't get out to buy all that stuff? I'd much rather have stall space, a little working space—and enough room to store a whole winter's supply of everything.

There are two ways to go about it. You can build your storage space alongside your stall—making the building just that much larger but no higher. Or you can build a two-story barn with a hipped roof—and all that room overhead—which, as I said, is considerably cheaper. Besides, hay stored overhead provides insulation and a surprising amount of warmth. And since not too many horses can climb stairs very handily, upstairs is a perfect place to store your grain, too. Most people who have only one horse store grain in a garbage can with a tight-fitting lid and assume that the horse, should it get loose some night and "head for the refrigerator," can't get into it. Well, just let me tell you, a horse can get into *anything,* if it has grain in it—with the possible exception of a steel vault fitted with a very complicated combination lock. So store your grain upstairs, if you can.

Whether you settle on a one-story or a two-story barn, there are some basic problems to think about. One is stall flooring, and you can start a

A brand-new horse barn, the kind everyone would love to have. Note the hipped roof for added storage space; the top-of-the-hill site for good drainage; and no snowdrift in front of the door. Good planning here. (Photo by John Dandelski, courtesy of Howard Turck.)

monumental debate about that. After all is said and done, though, I still like plain old dirt floors best. Clay floors are absolutely ideal, but you have to live where you can get the clay; so, barring that—earth. Dirt's biggest contender is probably cement, but while I personally don't know of a single barn that has cement stall floors, I can think of two or three places where the owners went to a great deal of expense to put them down, and then went to a lot more trouble and expense to remove or cover them.

Cement sounds ideal. It's easy to clean, and if it's sloped properly it drains nicely, too—all very neat and tidy-looking. However, for some reason, it's colder than dirt in the winter. It's also dangerously slippery, and it's so hard and unyielding that any horse kept on cement very long is quite likely to develop hoof, leg, even shoulder, stifle and hip problems. Cement just doesn't "give" at all. So if you insist on putting a cement floor in your horse's stall, you'll have to figure on using two or perhaps three times as much bedding, for warmth and for protection from all those ailments. This can be expensive in two ways—in paying for two or three times as much bedding, and in having to build two or three times as much storage space. In my opinion, it isn't worth it.

Another material sometimes used for flooring is very thick wooden planks, over either dirt or cement. I can't see any particular advantage to this kind of floor, except that the horse can't paw holes in it—and if you should get a pawer, I'll tell you later how to cramp his style, anyway! As for the old notion that rats can tunnel in through the dirt floors—there are plenty of safe, effective ways to deal with rats, so I wouldn't worry about them at this stage of the game.

Dirt floors don't look as pretty as cement floors. They look like *dirt,* is what they look like. But they'll be covered with nice clean bedding, and as far as I know, dirt floors never lamed a horse up or caused any practically incurable joint ailments—and your horse's health is far more important than mere prettiness. Your dirt or clay floor must be tamped down very thoroughly—hard work!—so that the surface is smooth, even, and as nonporous as dirt can be. It should also be sloped slightly toward a drain in one corner of the stall to prevent urine from pooling up.

Before we get on with this any further, and while you may still be looking around for something to remodel into a barn, I should say something about the old using-half-the-garage trick. Namely— don't do it. Use *all* the garage, if by some miracle you can get away with it and it's far enough away from the house. But don't plan on your horse's having a car for a roommate. The two just aren't compatible. Car fumes aren't any better for horses than they are for people, and "horse fumes" (ammonia and all that moisture) aren't good for cars. But even more important, it's asking for the worst kind of trouble to keep anything that's full of gasoline and that can cause sparks—like a car, a snowmobile or a lawn mower—in the same enclosed space as a horse stall full of highly flammable hay and sawdust or straw. Please don't plan on housing your horse in one end of the garage, then, unless you can also plan on permanently removing all motorized equipment and all possible fire hazards.

Now, having said all this, let me add that the possibilities for the actual construction or remodeling job are endless, ranging from a three-sided shed with a roof to a gorgeous brick stable. Which of these you'll eventually wind up with probably depends for the most part on two things: where you live (the milder the climate, the less elaborate the shelter need be) and how much money can be wangled for the project.

Obviously you yourself, with your own two hands, will not be constructing, let alone paying for, this project—at least not if it's all going to happen within the next year or two; so detailed, blueprint-type plans would be kind of silly here. I would like, though, to give you some idea of the basic requirements of a "one-horse horse house."

You will want your horse to have a box stall rather than a tie stall. Just put yourself in his place for a moment. A horse doesn't ask much out of life, really. Mainly, he wants plenty of good food, brought to him on time. Beyond that, he'd like plenty of tender loving care and a big clean stall so he can stretch his legs a little when for some reason he's confined to quarters. Now, is that asking a lot? Of course not. So plan for a stall about twelve by twelve feet for a full-sized horse, or about ten by ten for a pony or a very small horse. Anything larger than that, by the way, won't be that much harder to clean and will certainly be appreciated! As far as a horse is concerned, there's no such thing as a stall that's too big.

The height of the ceiling over the stall—the headroom—is important. Opinions on this vary somewhat, but I personally wouldn't feel very safe with much less than ten feet. Horses can't be counted on not to throw their heads up very suddenly when they're startled, or simply to start cutting up in the stall out of sheer boredom, high spirits and good health. The chances are that if he bumps his head once he won't do it again right away, but he *could* be severely injured. So allow all the headroom you can.

The leaning two-story old chicken house we turned into a two-horse barn (at about the same cost, I think, as building a new one a lot closer to the house—we live and learn) had an extremely low ceiling. My first horse and I were both exactly 15.1½ hands high, and we could just squeak under the center beam in the working area, but everyone else had to duck. Headroom that low was completely out of the question over the stalls, though, so we simply removed the ceiling in that end of the barn, making the stalls two stories high. The hayloft overhead, then, ended where the stalls began, which made "haying" very easy—I just dumped hay over the edge, usually on top of the horse, because he refused to move out of the way. And I never had to worry about Mark, the little Saddlebred gelding, bumping his head, even though he was unbelievably playful and active. Even *he* couldn't manage it.

And now for that storage space we've been talking so much about. Again, it isn't absolutely necessary. It's entirely possible to build a twelve-by-twelve-foot building with a door and a window or two, and put the horse in that, with a pile of sawdust and a pile of hay bales covered with tarps on the ground nearby. It'll work, if the hay doesn't get moldy and the sawdust doesn't get damp—and so will bringing in supplies a week's worth at a time. But it's a lot better all the way around if you can store that winter's supply of everything under one roof.

On the following page is a little diagram of what I consider to be the absolute minimum space required for one horse and a six-months' supply of hay and bedding. This, of course, is the first floor. On top of that should go the hipped roof we mentioned, so the hay can be stored

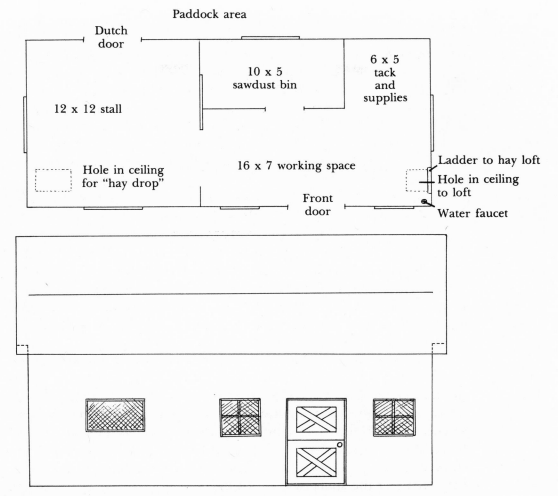

You can see from this sketch that you won't need a very large building if you have a hayloft overhead under a hipped or peaked roof. This is the minimum space for a one-horse operation.

upstairs. Either cut off the hayloft at the edge of the stall, as we did; or, if your ceiling is high enough, just cut a "hay drop" in it. And don't forget to put the grain can or bin upstairs, too. I keep harping on this because, while everybody knows it, I still keep hearing about yet another horse that "got into the grain last night," sometimes with no worse effects than that he wasn't hungry at breakfast time, but all too often with fatal results. You have to remember that most horses seem to be constantly looking for some way to eat themselves into a coma, and if there *is* a way, you can be sure they'll find it.

Now if, in spite of all my good advice, you aren't going to be able to go to two stories, you'll need another large room—about the size of two stalls—for hay storage and a sawdust bin. All the floors outside the stall can be cement. I'd strongly suggest that the floor marked "working space" in the sketch be outfitted with a drain, too, so you can wash the horse there—something you'll be doing a lot if you get into showing. And any cement floor where the horse will be standing, especially cross-tied, should be covered with a rubber mat. Nothing's much more heart-stopping than a horse that has slipped and gone down in the cross-ties.

If you're wondering why you'll need working space, just think about getting the horse's hooves trimmed or shod in the winter. It may not be strictly necessary to have a smooth, even surface for the farrier to work on, but it sure helps. Then, too, some winter day when your horse has been cooped up for a while and he's being especially playful and troublesome, you may well want someplace else to tie him out of your way while you clean his stall in peace. For quite a few reasons, a working space can be a real blessing now and then. Your cross-tie rings, by the way—and you should put some in the stall, too—must be extremely sturdy, as should your chains. A horse is incredibly strong. If you can't pull out the rings or break the chains with a tractor, then they're probably strong enough to hold a horse.

You'll notice that the diagram also shows a small area allotted for tack and supplies. It's probably too small, but in my experience, no matter how big it is, you'll soon have it full and overflowing. This is where you'll want to keep your tack in the summer (it might mold here in the winter), and where you'll have your cupboards, grooming box, tack trunk, and so on. A couple of large towel bars will also come in very handy for hanging coolers up neatly and for drying rubdown towels. But you'll find out what you want here as you go along. You can have a lot of fun designing this little area.

If you're a northerner, do you have to heat your barn? Before the winter of 1976–77, our worst and coldest in many years, I'd have said, "Never, never, never!" to artificial heat in a horse barn. *After* that winter, though, I have to say, "Well, *almost* never." For the first time in my life I heard about horses with frostbitten ears and muzzles, from the terrible cold-and-wind combinations. So maybe you should have a good, really safe, little portable heater on hand, just in case the temperature in your barn does take an awful drop—down to near zero, say. Otherwise, keeping a barn heated all winter long just makes your horse susceptible to all kinds of health problems and creates a totally unnecessary, intolerable fire hazard.

Finishing touches, now. Two modern conveniences that will save you a lot of time and make all your jobs much easier are electricity and plumbing. Neither one needs to be elaborate: a simple cold-water pipe with a faucet over in one corner of the work space, and some heavy-duty mouseproof wiring to provide adequate lighting and a socket or two for such things as clippers and submersible water heaters. Make sure the water pipe and the faucet are insulated, or wrapped with heater tape, in the winter, and if you have an overhead light in the stall, cover the bulb with heavy-gauge wire screening and box in the cables. Horses chew.

As to that—all horses seem to have been sired by beavers, so the wooden walls of the stall should be protected somehow. Painting the whole thing with creosote or some other deterrent before the horse even arrives might be a good idea. If you don't do something like that, and you get a really dedicated chewer, you might wind up creosoting the whole thing eventually anyway, bit by bit, as he works his way around the stall. Might as well do it all at once and get it over with.

If you weren't aware that horses chew, I have another little surprise for you. They also kick. And thin plywood just won't withstand a good, hearty, two-footed belt, so your stall walls should be made of hardwood at least two inches thick, bolted in place. And of course all barn windows, particularly stall windows, must have a heavy, securely fastened wire screen on the inside. (If all these precautionary measures are beginning to give you the idea that what a horse really needs is a padded cell, you're on the right track!) But by all means see that he does have windows in his stall. It'll make it more pleasant for *you*—it's hard enough to do a good job of stall cleaning without having to try to do it in the *dark,* for heaven's sake—and think of the horse, with nothing but knotholes to look at all day.

A wire screen for the upper half of your stall front will open it up and make it a great deal more pleasant than a solid wall. Vertical bars will serve the same purpose. (Photo by James Dandelski, courtesy of Holliday Farm.)

So much for windows. How about doors? All doorways, even those you don't intend to take the horse through, should be at least four feet wide, in case of emergency, and at least the standard six feet, eight inches high. Sliding doors are the handiest on inside stall doorways, and dutch doors are nice for the doorway between the stall and the paddock. Both should be equipped with a heavy hinged bar that can be raised or fastened firmly in place across the doorway. On the inside, between the stall and the work space, the door can be open to *you*—who can duck underneath—but closed to the horse—a great convenience. On the outside door, the bar gives the necessary added strength to the lower half of the dutch door—necessary because the horse will *lean* on it. When the bar is in place, especially when the door is otherwise wide open, it should be fastened from below with a couple of eye-rings, a short but sturdy chain, and a snap. Why? Because if it isn't fastened down, the horse will lift it up. (And don't ask me why he will lift it up—I have no idea why they do these things. I just know they *do* them!)

If you're going to have a barn and keep your horse at home, you'll also want some kind of fenced enclosure you can turn him out into. Not

No horse barn is complete without a resident mascot. If it happens to be a good mouser, so much the better. Horses love company and seem to enjoy cats in particular, a feeling that's usually reciprocated. (Photo by James Dandelski, courtesy of Holliday Farm.)

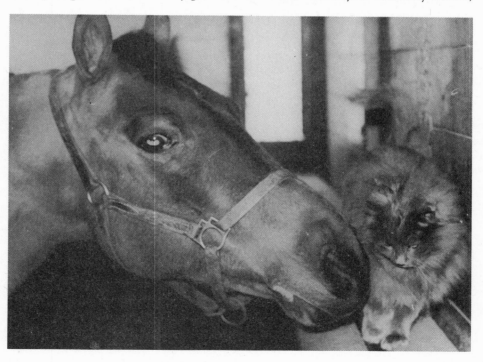

many people give a horse adequate exercise, so he'll need a place where he can "let his hair down" and romp and roll around, or just take a quiet little stroll. Remember that the smaller the paddock, the muddier it gets and stays; so fence in all you can. And try to arrange it so that in good weather you can leave the stall door open to allow the horse to come and go at will. This makes for great peace of mind, and he'll soon find the coolest, shadiest spot with the fewest flies.

Or a reasonably smart horse will. I had one horse that I always suspected of being a bit of a dim bulb, and one day he proved it. The dutch door was wide open and chained back against the outer barn wall so that it couldn't slam shut on him in the wind, leaving a shady, V-shaped angle between it and the wall. Inside the stall it was cool and comfortable, while outside it was blistering hot. And there stood Fella in the paddock. His entire body was exposed to that hot, hot sun—but his head was behind the door in the shade. Evidently he thought that if his head was cool, he must be cool, too. (Most horses are more intelligent than that, though—thank goodness.)

But let's get back to fencing. There are three basic kinds—wood, wire and rubber. Wood is the most expensive, but nothing beats a good, solid, three- or four-board fence for strength, safety and good looks. A woven-wire fence—the kind with "square holes" in it—costs less and is easier to install, but you do have to be a little concerned about it, as a horse can stick a leg through it and get hurt. Plain wire—and the very worst of all, barbed wire—is too dangerous by far. Your own horse may be a placid soul, but you never know when dogs, helicopters, or who-knows-what are going to send him into a panic and into a tangle of wire. My neighbor's two horses even took down a good-sized section of their split-rail fence one day when a helicopter got too close. Rubber fencing is relatively new. The best thing about it is, of course, that it would be hard for a horse to injure itself on it. On the other hand, I know of several local horses that had to be operated on to remove great wads of it from their insides! Chewing, again! So the word from here on fencing is: wood.

But what if you can't build a barn? Then you'll be looking for a good place to board your horse. Go back to Chapter One. If you found a nice place to learn about horses, as we described it there, then that's a good place to board. In any event, find out all you possibly can about the place and the people before you entrust your horse's health and well-being to them. Satisfied customers are a good clue; if they're happy, chances are you will be, too.

Remember that it's essential that your boarding barn be clean and well kept and that the people who run it are conscientious, caring, knowledgeable people. They should ask you to have your horse vetted before you bring it into their barn. This shows you that they know enough to *try*, anyway, to prevent an infectious disease from coming in. And it shows you that they're smart enough (and that they care enough) to keep a sharp eye on their boarders for any signs of trouble. It should be the kind of place where, if one horse coughs, they all get a shot when "there's something going around."

The stable I was describing to you earlier—my own favorite hangout—is a boarding as well as a training stable, and the owner is a capable riding instructor, too. A setup like this would be ideal for you. There's a large outdoor riding ring for good weather and a long, wide indoor riding hall for bad weather. Don't overlook this little detail when choosing a boarding stable, because if there's no place for you to ride, you won't get much use out of your horse. If you like trail riding, then there should be some safe, interesting trails adjacent to the place. In warmer climates an indoor hall or arena might not be so vital as it is up here in the North, but even in the deep South it might be nice to be able to ride in good footing when the outdoor ring is a sea of mud.

Some barns will offer "full board" only—you pay them so much a month and they take care of everything, including "maid service." Other barns only provide "bare board"; you have to do your own chores and perhaps even provide your horse's groceries. You'll just have to dig around for information, do some comparison shopping, and come up with the best deal you can. Some stables, I think, when they see how sincere you are, might be willing to let you "work off" at least some of the board.

How I wish I could tell you how much any of this is going to cost. But construction costs, feed prices, even boarding fees vary so wildly from place to place and from time to time that it's just not possible. Generally, though, boarding fees keep going up the closer you get to a sizable city, so those of you who live out in the country should have an easier time of it.

If whatever all this costs turns out to be just too much, why don't you look into the possibility of leasing a horse for a while instead of buying one? I know of several cases where this has worked out exceptionally well. So don't give up. Hang in there, and figure, and get out and earn some money. Buy your barn or shed board by board and nail by nail if you have to. Dedication such as yours must surely be rewarded—someday!

Chapter Four:
My Kingdom for a Horse

Almost always, the first question asked by the first-time horse buyer is, "How much does a horse cost?" The fact that it has no real answer doesn't keep it from being a very interesting one, so let's explore it a little.

Horsemen have a way of getting around this complex question, yet summing it all up very accurately, by saying that "any horse is worth exactly what somebody is willing to pay for it." Horses, unlike cars, have no "book value." You can't just look up the going price on a 1972 single-passenger quarter horse with a three-speed transmission, new shoes all around, like-new upholstery and only 200 miles on it. There's another quaint saying that "every horse in the barn is for sale," which means that every horse is available if the offer is high enough.

If you combine these two bits of wisdom, you'll see that it isn't usually a case of simply asking "How much?" and then paying that amount without even an argument. Or if it is, you're missing half the fun. A horse's seller has a pretty good idea of what *he* thinks it's worth, but he wants to know first what *you* think it's worth. And if you happen to appraise the animal a little more generously than he does, he certainly isn't going to put up much of a fight. So there can sometimes be a few tense moments. One of the hardest things about buying a horse can be, in fact, just trying to get a price out of somebody.

On the other hand, a horse will often have several prices, depending on who's asking. Is this "crooked"? Not especially. It's just accommodating today's price to what somebody is—or seems to be—willing to pay. This means that quite a few people end up paying more for a horse than perhaps they should have, but I can't see that as all bad. There's a psychological aspect to this that shouldn't be ignored. Look at it this way: you want to feel satisfied with your purchase; that's the main thing. If you have made up your mind that you are willing, able, even eager, to own a $1,000 horse, would you be satisfied with—or even bother to look at—a $500 horse, even if he was perfect for you? Probably not. And getting the right horse is much more important than paying the right price, as long as it's within your price range.

You really should have a range in mind. Make a firm decision about what you can pay, and then try to stick with it. This is always hard, and very often it isn't even possible. More than one person has started out looking for a $500 horse, come under a spell of some sort, and brought one home that cost several thousand. But if this is your first horse, and you've decided that $500 is plenty, you're probably right. That first horse, for most people, is in the nature of an experiment. So the best buy is the most horse you can find for what you can comfortably pay.

But what if you tell a dealer $500 and he then brings out Bourbon King's Springtime Whimsy, mumbling a figure that sounds alarmingly like $20,000? Don't walk out on him at that point. Maybe he just likes to trot out a good horse and show it off; most horsemen do. Enjoy it. Even a cat may look at a king. Or maybe the dealer, having run across a motley group of buyers, would-be buyers, and "just lookers" in his time, is just testing you out to see what you really want. Some people lie to a dealer about that, testing *him* out, although this is pointless. Other people are very sincere, but it turns out that what they think they want, and what they *need,* have no relation to each other at all. So how is the dealer to know? And, after all, it makes sense for him to start at the top. So that's all right. You'll see some wonderful horseflesh this way; and besides, maybe the next horse out of the stall will be Mr. (or Ms.) Right, to the inch and to the penny.

Actually, when it comes to price and to buying a horse in general, there's only one bit of advice that makes any sense at all: Find yourself an expert to help you. This could very well be somebody you've found at the barn where you hang out. In any event, he or she should be somebody you trust to know the horse business, somebody who knows exactly what your circumstances, abilities and requirements are. When you've had your fun playing horse trader and are starting to think about parting with some cash, put your expert to work on the problem.

Then, the *smartest* thing to do is leave him alone. Wait until he calls you up to tell you to come take a look at a likely prospect he's found. This takes a little of the fun out of it, but buying a horse can be an extremely emotional experience. Having your expert scout on ahead will help you to avoid falling in love with a horse at first sight, only to find later that you're stuck with one that's all wrong for you in every way there is. If your expert is as competent as he should be, he won't present you with any horses it wouldn't be safe to fall in love with.

Depending on your relationship with your expert (he may be a friend, a relative, or simply a dealer with a superb reputation), you should at least offer to pay him for his time, effort and expertise. A dealer or trainer usually receives about ten percent of the price, but whatever you pay—when you think of some of the horses you might have bought on your own—it's a bargain!

What do you tell your expert to look for? How do you know what you want in a horse? By this time you probably have a general idea, from all your reading and barn visiting and learning-by-doing. Also, you know now how well you can ride and how much horse you can be expected to handle capably. Make sure your expert is aware of all this. For example, if you're dead set on an Arabian and you know for sure that you want to ride and show saddle seat, and you really need a fairly well mannered, biddable horse, this will give your expert a lot to go on. It will save him from having to run down every for-sale ad in the paper or trucking around to Morgan barns.

At least he should know which breed you prefer. If you want to show in breed classes, you'll have to buy a purebred, of course; and the right specimen of any of the light breeds popular in this country can be ideal for you. It doesn't necessarily have to cost you any more than a good grade (crossbred) horse, either. Don't overlook the middle-aged purebred gelding or the occasional older barren mare. An aged, retired show gelding, as Mark was, usually isn't worth a whole lot of money, no matter how well he showed or how impeccable his bloodlines are, for the simple reason that he's sterile. Unlike a well-bred mare or stallion, he has no future, once his showing days are over. A horse that's just a bit too old for the hard training and campaigning required for showing may still have a lot going for him, too. Mark most assuredly didn't look or act either "aged" or "retired." In fact, I'm sure he wasn't aware of being either one.

A horse like Mark, of whatever breed, with several years of experience behind him as a show horse might be perfect for you to begin your riding and showing career. The fact that he's too old or that he is not of championship caliber and therefore not worth the terribly expensive professional training anymore is all in your favor, especially pricewise. You're not in a big rush to turn out a stake champion; you have all the time in the world, and you won't be expecting to win the big stake at Louisville with your first horse. (At least I hope you won't—for the kind of money we're talking about!) A big training stable's leftovers, also-rans and has-beens, in other words, can be ideal pickings.

So don't give up on your favorite breed just because you hear prices like $50,000 bandied about. Go to a few auctions where your breed is

The American Saddle Horse (Saddlebred) has often been called the most beautiful horse in the world. This picture of Society Rex, an influential breeding stallion, does nothing to dispute that statement. (Photo by John R. Horst, courtesy of the American Saddle Horse Breeders Association.)

Our representative of the Morgan horse is the lovely show mare Antoinette, Grand National Park Champion. The Morgan, very popular in the show ring, is also renowned for its versatility as an all-around pleasure horse. (Photo by Bob Moseder, courtesy of Larry Bolen, Cedar Creek Farm, Perrysburg, Ohio.)

This quarter horse, Snipper's Sarah, a halter champion, shows the broad, sturdy build and especially the heavily developed hindquarters of the breed. (Photo courtesy of the American Quarter Horse Association, Amarillo, Texas.)

Nevele Pride is a Standardbred. While Standardbreds are primarily intended for the harness racing tracks, a great many of them are serving well as riding horses. (Photo courtesy of the United States Trotting Association.)

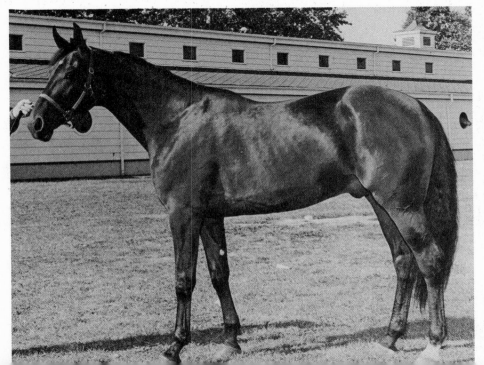

being sold—always leaving your money and your trailer at home! You'll soon see that some very nice stock is frequently sold for $1,000 or less, and not necessarily for "funny" reasons, either. People who raise and train show horses have awfully high standards, and what might be a mediocre horse to them might be a very, very good horse to you. Then go back to the auctions or around to the barns, with an expert who is well versed in that breed firmly in tow. With his help, I'll bet you'll find a well-trained, good-tempered horse that you can cope with.

Very few beginners can cope with a $50,000 stake horse, so you needn't feel deprived if you can't afford one. Perhaps this seems obvious to you, but far more beginners are over-mounted than under-mounted, by a long shot. This is too bad, because it's very discouraging to start out with a horse that's just too much for you to handle. This has put more than one person out of the horse business for good. It isn't even fair to the horse, who deserves better.

Now, if you're going to buy a purebred, how many breeds are there to choose from? Just counting the recognized light (riding) horse and pony breeds that are common in this country, there are eleven: Appaloosa, Arabian, Morgan, quarter horse, American Saddle Horse (often called Saddlebred), Shetland, Pony of the Americas (P.O.A.), Standardbred, Tennessee Walking Horse, Thoroughbred, and Welsh. It would be very easy here to fill up many pages with descriptions of these breeds and their breed traits, but as I've told you before, breed traits should be used only as general guidelines.

If you've read all your breed books and magazines thoroughly, you'll know as much as I do—or as much as most people do—about breed traits, anyway. And I want you to choose your first horse on its own merits rather than the merits of a lot of near and far relations. Choose a favorite breed, by all means, but then don't just run out and buy the first horse you come to that's registered in the right stud book. You might be lucky, if you do, and get just exactly what you expected to get—or you might be quite disappointed.

I think I can be more helpful by giving you some hints about choosing the right horse without regard to its bloodlines. Whatever breed you settle on, be sure you let your expert look first, or at least take him with you every time you go a-horse-hunting; and judge the horse very carefully for what it *is,* not what it's supposed to be, "according to the book."

For instance, no matter what breed you choose, or no breed—and there are countless crossbred horses of very high quality in this country—make sure he's the right size. You may well want a pony rather than a horse. Size isn't the most important thing about your new horse—or pony—but it can surely make a difference in how comfortable or uncomfortable you feel on it.

Shape is important, too. Many people don't think of this, but a small horse doesn't necessarily fit a small rider—not if the horse has a wide barrel. Take me: I'm five feet, one and half inches tall, and there are 15-hand horses I feel very uncomfortable on and 16-hand horses that feel just fine to me. Why should that be? Well, I'm short, and so are my legs. So when I'm sitting on a round-barreled horse (totally regardless of how long *his* legs are), my knees hit him just above his widest part. That leaves my lower legs sticking outward, and I feel as though I can't "get around" him. I know you're not supposed to "clutch" a horse with your lower legs, but those legs should at least be able to point in the general direction of the ground!

On a narrower horse, on the other hand, my little short legs have a chance. I may have an awful time getting up there, but, once in the saddle, I can feel horse with my lower legs instead of just air. So don't judge a horse's size by height alone. Even if he looks about right, you'll have to get on him, ride him around awhile, and find out how he feels to you. There's something about not being able to get your legs close to a horse that makes *me*, anyway, feel insecure. None of this would make a bit of difference to an old hand who can ride anything, but beginners need all the help they can get.

Then there's the matter of gender: which one, or none at all, in the case of geldings. You already know how I feel about stallions—they can be wonderful, but they're not usually recommended for beginners' pets. Besides, if they were really good enough to have remained ungelded, then they should be in somebody's breeding program. And if they weren't good enough, then I don't know why they weren't gelded, if only for their own peace of mind.

So if I were you, I'd limit my choice to mares and geldings. And here again, judge each horse separately, because it's hard to generalize. Some mares become extremely difficult when they come in season (their times for breeding), which is really only every two to four weeks but can *seem* like every other day. Such mares are to be avoided, if possible—if you can find out about it—because some of them actually undergo a personality change and get downright nasty. Most mares, though, get through their seasons with very little change in behavior, many with none. Oh, they may stand in the stall and absentmindedly thump a hip against a wall, but they won't go out of their minds or anything.

Some trainers are prejudiced against mares, claiming they're too "notional"—that is, quirky and unreliable. Well, we girls are used to that kind of talk. And other trainers claim mares are easier to work with because they're smarter! Maybe some trainers just don't get along with women as well as others do.

And geldings? They're supposed to be milder in temperament than either stallions or mares. But here again, all you have to do is hang around a few training and boarding stables to learn that it's another case of "some is; some isn't." What it boils down to is that some geldings are better tempered than some mares, and some mares are better tempered than some geldings. On the average, perhaps, geldings are more dependably good natured and less flighty than mares. But as long as you don't get one of the few mares that act up when they're in season, I don't think you have to be overwhelmingly concerned about this, if you're careful to choose a horse with a nice disposition.

Neither do you have to be too terribly concerned about the fine points of conformation. It takes a lot of experience and observation to become adept at judging a horse, anyway. It wouldn't do any harm to be aware of a few of the major faults, though, those anybody can see right away. You don't want a horse with really bad legs, for instance. Such a serious conformation fault can mean trouble. "Cow hocks" that point toward each other are a weakness, as are severely bowed hindlegs that make it look as though the horse's tail is in parentheses! A horse that's "over at the knee"—the knee joint juts forward of the lower leg—can mean trouble, too. Seabiscuit won many a stake race on a pair of knees like that, but not *because* of them. A horse with straight (too vertical) shoulders or short, stumpy, straight pasterns ("ankles") might not only give you a rough ride but turn up lame a lot, too, because these conformation faults deprive him of good shock absorbers.

Many faults, though, are more a matter of unattractiveness than of unsoundness and are only as important as they seem to *you*. "Beauty is only skin deep," and "pretty is as pretty does." Many a homely horse is considered very handsome by a loving owner. But I rather like to see a pretty face when I've struggled to the barn in the morning, and a good-looking horse doesn't eat any more than an ugly one, so you might as well try to find a horse whose appearance pleases you. Otherwise, you can leave this up to your expert, because it's really his department.

You do have to be very concerned about temperament and training, however. I think of these two together, because usually a bad temperament is the result of incompetent, sometimes even abusive handling. Maybe some horses do inherit a certain predisposition to "being cross," but by and large a foal comes into the world ready to be friendly if he's given a chance. Temperament and training can be judged only when you've been around the horse for a while. Ideally you should buy a horse you've already been able to observe, work around, and ride for some time, as at your favorite stable. Barring that, try for a free trial period. You may not be given one, however, because these days everyone's so liability- and lawsuit-conscious. Maybe the best you'll be able to do is keep on the lookout for indications.

As a sterling example, there was one horse whose looks I didn't like at all the first time I went to see him. I just had the feeling that he was grumpy. After thinking it over a day or two, I decided that since he was the first one I'd seen thus far that wasn't skinny or horribly misshapen, and since he had had a little training—all for $200—I'd better buy him. It turned out that I was right the first time. My instincts, or whatever it was that told me so, were correct.

He was a lazy, sneaky little horse, and that can be the most frustrating kind. (This was Fella, by the way, the buckskin that put his head behind the door to get cool!) Oddly enough, I didn't find out all this about him until after I'd sold him. All the while I kept him he behaved himself, basically, but that must have been because all the while I had him, he pretty much had his own way about everything. But when somebody got hold of him who really asked him to *do* something, all his little tricks came into play. Yet even while I owned him, I had this feeling about him. He didn't kick or bite or anything else, but I just couldn't like him. Moreover—and even worse—I always felt that he didn't especially care for me, either. That's why I finally sold him. How unrewarding! Going to all that work and expense for a horse you don't even *like*. So sometimes it's a matter of pure instinct. If someone ever tries to sell you a horse that you feel this way about, don't buy it under any circumstances. You have to *love* your horse, above all else.

Another indication of a horse's temperament is the way people act around it. Are they telling you how kind and gentle he is, without for an instant taking their eyes off his heels? Do they handle the horse with kid gloves, or doesn't he mind a casual, hearty, unexpected slap on the neck? Sometimes sensitivity is a good thing—a certain amount of it always is—but a supersensitive horse might find life with a beginner too traumatic. A certain amount of tolerance is a good thing, too, because your horse may have to tolerate a good many mistakes on your part!

Your first horse must be good-natured, then; not too awfully sensitive; and well trained, especially if *you're* not yet. After all, one of you had better know what you're doing. This rules out most very young horses; it takes time to train a horse well. It also rules out horses "trained" by other kids who don't know any more than you do about it, and it rules out horses trained by adults who only think they know how. And, by all means, it rules out horses trained by show-offs, whatever their age. Somebody, for instance, who thinks it's great fun to teach a horse to take off like a bat the instant a foot touches the stirrup. It's only great fun if you don't mind being dragged for miles by one foot, or having your head stomped on repeatedly.

So do find out, if you can, who trained your horse. If you can't, make sure your expert really puts it through its paces, including trying to find out what it's scared of, before you decide anything. (A horse that remembers its manners even when it's scared half out of its shoes is well trained.) This is another good reason for considering a former show horse. Few horses are better trained than show horses; by the time they've been on the circuit a few years, not much frightens them; and most of them are professionally trained by people who for the most part do know what they're doing.

Perhaps you've noticed that I haven't even mentioned color here as something to look for. Well, I know that when you're fantasizing about your horse, its color is very important to you. But in real life, when you're actually buying a horse, the color is the *last* thing you have to worry about. There are superstitions and prejudices galore about horse colors, but the truth probably is that whether a horse is jet black, pure white or mud brown has no bearing whatever on its temperament, training, or anything else except its appearance. Think about color if you absolutely can't help it, but don't let it have any real influence on your decision. If your horse is right for you in all the important respects, you're going to love him no matter what hue he sports. I have a book, *Every Horse Owners Cyclopedia,* published in 1870, that puts it extremely well. "A good horse," it says, "is always the right color." Amen to that.

Once you've hunted down a horse that's the right breed or type, the right size and shape, with the right temperament and training, *and* your expert tells you it's probably really Mr. Right—call the vet at once, before you buy. Then try not to get too excited until you hear his verdict. A great many horses, especially those over nine or ten, do have something wrong with them, but you don't want a horse with navicular disease, for instance, or with an advanced case of emphysema, or any real leg or foot problems. The vet will explain any faults he finds and will advise you as to the probable difficulties they indicate. If the prognosis isn't good, then you will just have to put that horse out of your mind and get busy right away finding another one. As time goes on you'll have enough troubles, in the natural course of events, but there's no sense in *buying* a batch of them. It's heartbreaking to have to turn a horse down after you think you've fallen in love with it, but not nearly so heartbreaking as buying one with serious health problems.

When you have your horse vetted, you'd better find out about all the current laws on inoculations for infectious diseases. The vet will know what your state's requirements are, and the requirements for crossing state lines if you've gone far afield. And while you're at it, if he gives your horse a passing grade, you can set up a schedule for future inoculations.

Remember one more thing, please. You can't be too careful, or take too long, to find the right horse. Try not to be impatient, and give your expert plenty of time. It might be only a matter of weeks, but it could be months before the right horse comes up for sale. But which would you really rather have: the wrong horse right now, or the right horse in a little while? And just about the time you begin to feel discouraged, somebody will lead out a horse that you just know was born to be yours.

It's a moment well worth waiting for.

Chapter Five:
The Great Jack Hunt

Now your brand-new horse is installed, literally, in your brand-new or remodeled barn or shed or boarding stable, and it's time to think about "horse furnishings." Your tack (saddlery) will take the biggest bite out of your budget, so use care. By this time, I hope, you know which seat you'll be riding—hunt, stock or saddle seat—and will have bought your horse accordingly. Buy your tack accordingly, too. Presumably any kind of horse can be ridden any seat with any kind of tack. But if you've bought a nice hunter, you'll probably want to ride him hunt seat, for instance. Some kinds of horses and tack just naturally go together. And if you plan to get into showing, of course your tack has to be appropriate to your classes.

Whatever style you've settled on (more about that later), you can go out and buy a brand-new saddle and bridle if you have the means; or, if you want to economize, you can find yourself a good used set. You *can* economize this way without necessarily sacrificing quality or durability, since many of the saddles that come up for sale have had very little use. Some, even, that show lots of use are still good buys because they were so well made to begin with. A really good saddler's product is meant to last at least one person's lifetime, and with good care many outlast several owners. Some asking around will give you the names of the best saddlers, and you would be well advised to stick to those brand names. An off-brand saddle might hold up with light use, or it might come apart at the staples (yes, some of them are stapled together!) at the worst possible moment.

Finding good used tack might mean rummaging around for some time in people's tack rooms, haylofts, and sheds out back. It depends. If you're going to ride stock seat, or western, as it's often called, and a lot of other people in your area ride western, you might find a good used saddle very easily. But if you decide on a style that's not particularly popular where you live, you may have to look further afield and it may take a while longer.

44

No matter what kind of horse you choose, you'll have some choice as to tack. Here are two Walking Horses: one all ready to go, saddle seat; the other in a stock saddle. Both are wearing Walking Horse bridles and bits. (Photo courtesy of the Tennessee Walking Horse Breeders' & Exhibitors' Association.)

You can combine projects as I did, though, to save time and effort. While I was attending an out-of-state show for a few days, I was also going to barns in that area which had for sale the kind of horses I was interested in, and at the same time, I was keeping an eye out for a used saddle. I found one at a barn that was showing me a horse. Luckily, my expert was along. We turned down the horse but positively grabbed the saddle, after hauling it out of a pile of other dusty old stuff and brushing off the cobwebs.

It didn't look like much at the time, and if my friend hadn't been with me I know I wouldn't have given it a second look. It had no fittings at all (girth and stirrup leathers and irons), and the pads underneath were shot, but when it came back from the saddler's with new fittings and new calfskin pads it was beautiful. And it had cost me only one-third to one-half the price of a new saddle with that respected brand name.

This little story also points out another thing to keep in mind. If you buy good quality and condition, regardless of age, your saddle will virtually never depreciate as long as you own it if you *care* for it. One reason is the longevity of a good saddle, and the other is that new tack goes up in price continually—inflation! So take very good care of your saddle, so that some day somebody like me won't be able to pick it up cheap because it *looks* so bad.

Ordinarily you should do as I say and not as I did, and buy your horse before you buy a saddle for him, to make sure it will fit him. But with my experienced friend along who knew what size (and shape!) horse I needed, I was safe enough. Also, I had the added advantage of buying saddle seat, which is easier to fit to most horses. Hunt seat saddles and stock saddles are usually more difficult, so you'll have to be more careful about fitting those.

Bring the saddle home for a try-on before you say you'll buy it. Whatever kind it is, if there are a lot of gaps between it and the horse that can't easily be filled in with a thin pad, or any places that pinch, rub, or cut into his flesh, try another one. A saddle that perches up on his withers or has to be positioned awkwardly to fit at all won't work either. And don't forget that there are two of you to consider. Your horse must be comfortable to do a good job for you, and you'll feel a lot better if you're comfortable, too.

Saddles are made in different sizes for different horses and ponies, and in different sizes for different people. The size is referred to in inches, which in turn refers to seat length, from front to back. An average size for a saddle seat saddle is probably twenty-one inches. This is the measurement from the tiny metal "nailhead" on the side of the pommel to the center of the rear edge of the cantle. My own saddle is only nineteen inches. I wish I could say that this is because I have such a small "seat," but what you have to consider is the length of your legs, not the size of your posterior. This may sound strange, but it's really quite obvious. If your legs are short, and you're wearing your stirrup leathers correctly, your seat just doesn't sit as far back on the horse as that of someone whose legs are long. And that's important, so when you're trying a saddle on your horse, be sure to take that ride. Ride long enough to overcome the initial feeling of strangeness, so you'll really know whether the saddle feels good or not. If possible, have your expert or your friends at the barn give their opinions on how you look, too. If you look comfortable, as well as feel right, chances are pretty good that the saddle fits you. They should also advise you on the quality and condition of any used tack you're thinking about buying. This can be difficult for a novice to judge accurately.

Used bridles may be harder to find, and I think it's harder to judge how strong they still are. So you might want to spring for a new one, unless you happen to luck into a fairly new one that can be fitted well to your horse. Having a bridle fall apart while you're riding is no more enchanting than having a saddle come to pieces. The fitting of the bridle is another job best left to your expert. If it isn't done exactly right, you can cause your horse discomfort or even pain, to the point where he might exhibit all sorts of mysterious behavior just because his mouth or ear is being hurt. The bit or bits you use must also fit perfectly and be positioned properly.

Regardless of what kind of bitting you and your experts decide will be appropriate for your horse, if he's been used to something entirely different, you'd probably better use it for a while. He should have time to get well acquainted with you and to settle into his new life. A change of bitting can be quite traumatic to a horse if he has to cope with it on top of a lot of other unsettling circumstances. Wait awhile, and then make the change gently.

Sometimes a horse will be advertised for sale "with saddle and bridle." Don't get all excited about it. It might be a good deal for you and it might not. A great many horses are running around the countryside wearing very ill-fitting tack, so go through your whole fitting routine even if the horse has been wearing that saddle for years—*especially* if you see any bald, sore or white-haired patches on his saddle area. And again—make sure that any "included" tack fits you, as well. If it doesn't, there's no point in hauling it home—unless it's in good shape but just badly in need of some saddle soap and elbow grease and you think you can clean it up and make some money on it. That's kind of fun to do, and anything that will help pay for the saddle you buy to use might be welcome.

Now, a saddle and a bridle are essential. I rode old Kate bareback, with a work bridle and a piece of clothesline, but no one would call that very safe. (I did a lot of things when I was younger that I would never advise you to do—or even admit to!) What else, then, do you really need in the way of tack? Well, some horses need special gear like a martingale, heel boots, and so on, but the average horse doesn't. A good sturdy halter, though, is one thing that every horse needs. A horse usually comes with a halter, but it's almost always some old thing that the seller dug around for in his junk pile, frayed and just about to pull apart. Make sure your horse is outfitted with not one but two strong halters. They don't have to be big clunky things to be strong, but the leather or nylon must be in good shape, and they should be stitched together, never riveted. Why so strong, and why two?

Because horses do some pretty nutty things, and one of them is now and then to destroy a halter. I went into Mark's stall one morning and found his halter dangling from around his little ears. The snap that had fastened it under his jowls had broken in two. Now, when I built that stall for him I made doubly sure that there was nothing he could catch his halter on. Not his feed or water containers, not the eye-bolts for his cross-ties—*nothing*. Yet there the halter dangled.

I finally concluded that the only possible way he could have done it

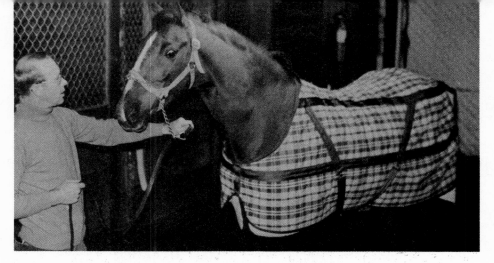

Scarlet Angel models her new plaid top blanket; underneath she wears a smooth white one. Sheets and blankets not only keep the horse warm and short-coated; they also cut down considerably on grooming time, since the horse stays much cleaner. (Photo by James Dandelski, courtesy of Holliday Farm.)

was to stick a hind foot up there—scratching his ear, probably—and to somehow manage to catch the edge of his hoof or shoe behind that strap. Just think of the strength required to break a heavy brass snap in two. And then think what might have happened if it had *not* broken and his hoof had been *really* stuck! At best, I'd have found a panic-stricken horse in that stall, and at worst—well, I can't bear to think about it. Close calls like this explain all those gray-haired young horsemen. But don't conclude from this experience that a halter should be weak so that it will break. Ninety-nine times out of a hundred, it's much better if the halter *doesn't* break. In fact, ninety-nine times out of a hundred, I doubt that a horse could break any halter with his hind foot; Mark was just very clever! But your horse might be very clever, too, so you'll need a standby halter, to put on while you're getting the other one repaired.

You may or may not want "clothing" for your horse—sheets and blankets. If you show him you'll probably keep a sheet on him in the summer to keep his coat smooth, and a blanket or blankets in the winter to keep it short. Or you might want to keep him blanketed in the winter so you can ride and exercise him harder without having to take all day to cool him out afterward. Otherwise, it's a matter of your own personal preference—whether you like shaggy horses or not—and how well you like to do laundry. (Very dirty laundry!)

I've often read that fine-coated, "delicate horses" like Saddlebreds and Thoroughbreds absolutely require clothing in cold winters, especially if they're kept in a one-horse barn without the benefit of the body heat of several other horses to warm the place up. I believed it, until I had Mark. A finer coated horse doesn't exist, and, being so small and fine boned, he even looked fragile and "delicate." As long as he was still at the trainer's barn, in the summer, he wore a sheet—as much to keep the flies from bothering him as anything. But after he came to my own little barn he went around stark naked. This was in November—an especially cold, wet November—and as it got colder and colder I worried more and more. I needn't have. He quickly grew his own bright red winter coat. It wasn't very long, and it was extremely fine, but it was thick and plush. In fact, it looked and felt rather like sheared beaver. And although on one memorable morning the inside barn thermometer registered thirteen degrees above zero, I never once saw Mark look to be anything but very comfortable and extremely bright eyed and bushy tailed. Not a shiver, a sniffle or a cough, all that terrible winter.

On the other hand, if I had started out the winter by keeping him covered so that he hadn't had a chance to grow his own winter coat, I'd have been obliged to keep it up, adding layers of blankets as it got colder. It can be dangerous to interfere with nature without following through on it. It can be just as dangerous to run out there with a blanket in the middle of the winter when he isn't used to one. So when you decide, one way or the other, stick with your decision. And be warned that some horses can't tolerate wool next to their hides. You'll need a cotton or nylon sheet for "underwear," in that case, and two or three heavy wool blankets to go on top of it. A heavy canvas or duck blanket is nice on the very top, too; it's easier to brush off clean. Good blankets are very expensive, so you might see what you can do about scrounging some used ones.

Whether you blanket or not, you'll need a couple of coolers: a very lightweight one for summer and one of very heavy wool for winter. The whole idea is to keep a horse from cooling out too rapidly, and obviously the colder the air temperature, the more protection he'll need. There are even times when a show horse in winter training will need to spend the rest of the entire day under two heavy wool coolers to cool out safely, but I wouldn't recommend that you work your horse that hard or long in cold weather since you won't really have to.

When the weather breaks after your horse has been cooped up for a long time, and you let him out into his paddock, he may work *himself* into a sweat, just because he's so tickled at the chance to stretch his legs. Have a cooler ready for him when he gets through playing. You could save his life. I know I told you that in nature horses don't usually move around very much or very fast in winter, but one that's been suffering from cabin fever is quite likely to do both!

Your horse is all outfitted with the necessaries now, and perhaps even a summer and a winter wardrobe, and all that remains is to fill up your tack-and-supplies corner with the rest of the gear you'll need to get started with. When you're shopping, a lot of fancy knickknacks will catch your eye, but concentrate on what you need. If you still have some nickels left after you've bought all *that,* then fine.

Even if you're boarding your horse at a stable, it's always better not to borrow brushes and whatnot. For your grooming box and corner of the tack room, you'll need a hoof pick for digging mud, stones, packed sawdust and other trash out of your horse's hooves; a halter shank, which is a strong leather strap with a twenty-inch brass chain and snap at one end; a couple of rolls of leg bandage for trailering or the occasional injury and lameness; plenty of big safety pins, for all sorts of things; a soft brush and a coarser brush, small enough to fit your hands comfortably; a flexible rubber or plastic currycomb; a sweat scraper with a toothed shedding blade on one side; a couple of good-sized pails; a large natural sponge; and as many old bath towels as you can possibly beg from your mother and all your friends.

If you're keeping your horse at home, you'll need a small hand sprayer for fly spray, too, and you can also find use for electric hair

We set this up to show you how very little space is needed for all your gear. A wooden tack rack like this one will hold everything neatly in one small area, whether in the tack corner of your barn or, as here, in the house in the winter. (Photo by John Dandelski.)

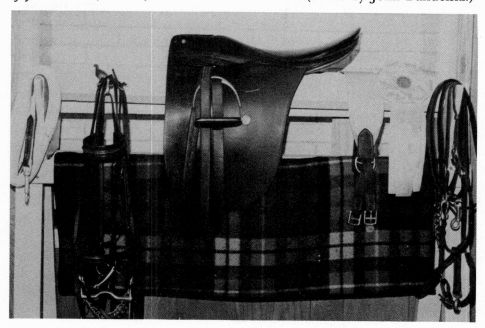

clippers, but they're so expensive that I'd certainly see if I couldn't borrow somebody's before I'd buy them just for occasional use on one horse. You'll be wanting warm water when you bathe your horse, so an immersible water heater that you plug in and set in a pail of water might come in handy, and it won't cost much. (The very idea of them scares the wits out of me, though, so *I'd* be inclined just to run to the house for a pail of hot water!)

This just about takes care of your supply corner for the moment, but if you haven't quite finished furnishing your horse's stall yet, you might buy a rubber corner bucket for his water. In fact, buy two, so in the winter you can just trade him a bucket of water for a bucket of ice instead of having to thaw it out right then and there. "Rubber" (this is a special heavy-duty rubber) so that if he does happen to bash into it he won't be likely to hurt himself; "corner" so that he'll be less likely to bash into it no matter how abandoned he gets. The best of these has a special patented fastening that is supposed to prevent a horse from removing the bucket from the wall. It usually works. They weren't reckoning on bored, inventive little Mark, however, who not only removed it almost instantly; he also kicked it around his stall for a while and then, judging from its shape when I rescued it, *sat* on it.

In another corner of the stall, put a strong vinyl-plastic corner grain container. This is for safety as well as for ease in cleaning (it can be removed), and again, there's a snazzy little edge around the top that's supposed to prevent a horse from wasting his grain by nosing it out onto the floor. And *again,* Mark outfoxed them. He was such an eager eater, and got so excited about it, that he sprayed grain wildly in all directions. I finally had to give him about half again as much as he really *ate,* to allow for the "spray" I had to brush off his back. (These little stories I'm telling you are in the nature of warnings. No matter what "the book"—this or any other book—says, a horse is always full of little surprises.)

Speaking of little surprises, you'll be finding piles of them in the stall every day—an average of fifty pounds' worth. So buy a wheelbarrow or a large basket or washtub, whichever means you prefer to use to lug the stuff out and bring fresh bedding in. For this little chore you'll also need a manure fork and a large aluminum sawdust shovel. If you can find a lightweight manure fork, I'd be much obliged if you'd write and tell me where you got it, because every one I've ever operated has weighed a *ton,* for some reason.

At this point you may be suspecting that a horse requires a certain amount of exhausting effort.

Your suspicion is about to be confirmed.

Chapter Six: Choretime!

Fundamentally, there are three things that'll get you through choretimes successfully. First of all, your attitude. I think I can take for granted that you love horses very much and that you love to work around them. As much as I despise housework, I couldn't be happier than when I'm cleaning out a horse stall. Many's the time I've industriously swept down cobwebs in the barn, while they collected in perfect safety in the house. But when it was bitter, bitter cold, even I wasn't always that cheerful about the prospect of leaving the warm house and staggering over to the barn against a killing wind at seven-thirty in the morning. The prospect of Mark's ecstatic greeting always pulled me through, though. He always made me feel like a real hero.

But you're younger than I am, and you probably don't hate winter as much as I do. Even so, you should be fully aware before you start that a horse is a full-time responsibility. You don't feed a horse when you have time; you feed it *on* time. Two or three times a day, seven days a week, fifty-two weeks a year. Only if you're lucky enough to know a reliable, willing horse-sitter will you be able to go away even for a weekend, without your horse in the trailer behind you, ever again. And if this is to be your horse, you are the one who should take care of it. Don't count on your parents or your little brother or anyone else to do it for you unless you're absolutely out of commission. The quickest way I know of to lose your privilege of having a horse is to duck the accompanying responsibilities. Being so terribly aware of all this responsibility needn't take any of the enjoyment away, though. There's really something very nice about knowing that a living, loving creature depends on you, and then never letting him down.

The right attitude then amounts to: (1) loving to do it most of the time; (2) knowing you *have* to do it the rest of the time; and (3) just going ahead and doing it, without even considering any other possibilities.

The second fundamental thing—and this will help you out with your attitude, too—is *routine*. Anything is always easier to do, even with a sick headache, if it's so routine that you don't have to figure it out as you go along. Doing chores should soon become a habit. Then, at the odd times when it really isn't all that enjoyable, you don't notice it so much. You'll hardly even know you've done them.

Allow fifteen or twenty minutes, just at first (you'll speed up as you go along), for feeding and watering the horse in the morning, and get up that much earlier. I'd suggest you do chores first thing, before you bathe and dress for school, if you don't want to be known as Old Barnsmell. Morning chores are minimal—water, hay and grain, in that order. No matter how glad your horse is to see you, he'll want to be left alone to eat his breakfast in peace, anyway, so you don't have to clean the stall then.

Remember that everything is likely to take longer in the winter. For instance, if you have only one stall bucket, instead of just filling it, you'll have to take it out, run warm water over the outside of it to loosen up the solid block of ice, dump it out, fill the bucket with water, and put it back. This means that if you're carrying water from the house, you'll need two pailfuls instead of one—one for thawing and the other for filling. (Some barns have quite a sizable pile of giant round ice cubes just outside the door, some winters.)

Then give him his morning ration of hay, and then his grain. The theory behind this sequence is that the horse will drink some water first (and in the winter, with an ice bucket instead of a water bucket, he may be thirsty), then will eat a little hay, and then will eat his grain, thereby avoiding eating grain first and then flushing it all through with water. In practice, though, in a one-horse barn, one step follows the other so closely that it doesn't seem to make that much difference, unless you can wait around for half an hour or so while all this takes place. Even then, Mark wouldn't even look at hay when he knew for certain there was grain coming up next. But that's the theory anyway, and it doesn't do any harm to try it.

How much should you feed him? Ask your expert. I can't tell you, because I don't know how big your horse is, whether he's an easy keeper or hard to fatten up (that buckskin I had stayed overly plump on dry leaves that blew into the paddock, while Mark could consume great quantities of feed without gaining an ounce), or how hard he'll be working. So find out from your experienced friends who know your horse. Then if he seems to be getting too rotund, or too chipper to handle, cut him back. Just play it by ear. In the winter, when a horse can't get out to let off steam as often as both of you would like, you might have to cut him back just to keep him from demolishing his house.

Whenever you're in doubt, ask somebody who knows. Unfortunately, we still hear about undernourished, even starving horses, but most people err on the side of generosity, considering it a kindness; and overfeeding is just as bad, in its own way, as underfeeding. Too much hay, for instance, can give your horse a ridiculous potbelly that's known, reasonably enough, as a hay belly. (I once heard a lady say that her horse had a beer belly, though, which I sincerely hope was just a slip of the tongue.) Too much grain is even worse, and grossly overfeeding grain can lead to colic, which is sometimes fatal and always frightening; or to foundering, which is usually crippling. Good clean fresh water, of course, should be available "free choice" to your horse at all times (except when he's overheated), even if it soon becomes a block of ice. At least he can *lick* it, and Mark used to break his into little bits somehow, whereupon, presumably, he chewed it up.

More about feed in a little bit, but right now let's get your schedule underway. In the summer or on weekends, when you're not in school, you should make a trip to the barn around noon, even if you're only feeding twice a day, as I did. (That's usually enough, unless you're trying to build up an undernourished animal.) At noon, or any time during the day except near feeding time, you can clean the stall and do your grooming and fussing, without having your horse jump up and down on you and carry on because he thinks you're going to feed him any minute. You may want to do this just before or just after riding.

On school days you'll probably find it more convenient to clean the stall, change the bedding, and groom the horse right after school. If you wait any later, you're starting to run into feeding time, and after that it's often getting dark. Whatever time you decide on for your barnwork and feedings, you must make it a set routine. Horses are such creatures of habit that they can actually get quite upset if their little routine is changed, and even if they're not that sensitive, they probably do better—stay in better condition—on a schedule. Don't let anyone ever try to tell you that a horse doesn't know exactly what time of day it is, either. At four sharp every afternoon Mark used to start battering his stall walls—and even Fella was standing in a particular corner of the paddock—because it was close to food time, the highlight of their day. And over at my favorite stable it's the same thing. Comes four o'clock, and the barnful of horses start whinnying, kicking and in general making sure nobody forgets. They have clocks in their stomachs.

The grooming of your horse can become a routine in itself. There will be summer days when you'll want to take an hour or so to primp and bathe him and just enjoy his company. But for the days when you're

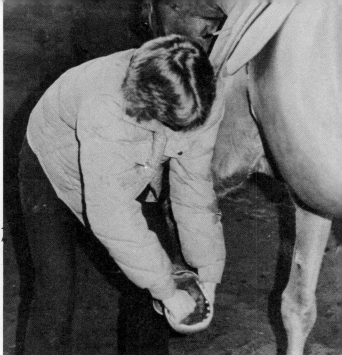

(LEFT) Bathing an animal the size of a horse can be a wet operation. In this case, quite obviously, a good time is being had by all, but it might be wise to wear a swimsuit! (Photo by Lois Rappaport, courtesy of the American Saddle Horse Breeders Association.) *(RIGHT) Hoof cleaning is a daily necessity, and it doesn't do any harm to pick out the hooves again before and after riding. Sawdust and other matter can pack up and become very uncomfortable. Notice that Sally is standing well out of the way, in case her gelding, Squire Hall, forgets she's there and kicks at a fly.* (Photo by James Dandelski, courtesy of Holliday Farm.)

rushed, get it all down to a science. First, the minimum requirements, to be done every day: The hooves should be cleaned out with a hoof pick and inspected for any signs of trouble, unless he's wearing pads. Make even this a routine. Start with the near (left) fore, for instance, then go to the near hind, and so on around. Mark taught me *his* routine on this, picking up his feet in the sequence he was used to. This will speed things up considerably, because soon your horse, too, will be lifting the next hoof on the agenda before you even reach for it, instead of your having to tug and plead every time.

Stand close to the leg you're interested in at the moment, facing the horse's rear. Bending down, run your hand down the leg to the pastern, and tell your horse what you want, which is for him to cooperate by lifting his hoof. If nothing happens, tap the front of the pastern and pull gently at the fetlock. You might even have to lean on him a little, to get him to shift his weight off that leg. But that should be *all* you'll have to do. We'll assume that your expert didn't let you get stuck with a horse

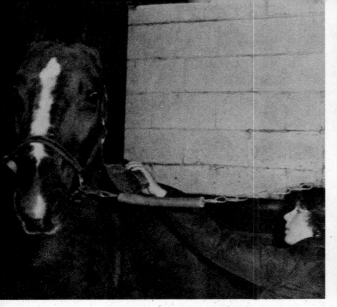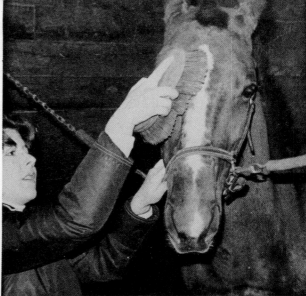

(LEFT) Your grooming routine will be much easier and safer if you cross-tie your horse. The rubber tubing "sleeves" prevent the horse from being scratched or pinched, should he decide to nibble at the tie chains. (RIGHT) Use a cloth or only the softest brush on your horse's face. Since Susie doesn't want Pinwheel's Scarlet Angel to become head-shy, she is using great care not to hurt her. (Photos by James Dandelski, courtesy of Holliday Farm.)

that refuses to let you work with his feet, as this is pretty basic training, and it's essential to your horse's health. You can use a little hoof dressing afterward if your expert says your horse needs it, but use it sparingly.

Once the hooves are picked out, you can brush him. You'll want to use just a soft brush in the summer, but a stiffer one might be needed for the coarser, longer winter hair. A mane comb isn't necessary; brush the mane and tail lightly (so as not to pull out too many hairs and leave them scraggly looking), and, before a show, separate the hairs by hand to fluff them, and use a little dressing to make them shine.

They say that a well-kept horse will never need a currycomb, but once in a while yours might, if he has soiled his coat by lying in manure. Let the manure dry, loosen it gently with the currycomb, and then brush his coat like mad. You might be lucky enough to get a fastidious horse like Mark, who made precise little piles in a certain corner and never got dirty; or you might get one like Fat Albert, the cream-colored gelding. If there was one little bit of manure within a hundred miles, he'd be sure to take his afternoon nap right on top of it. So you'd better have a currycomb, just in case!

Most horses seem to enjoy a good hard brushing, and that's what it takes to get them really clean, to give them a good massage, and to help tone up their muscles. But remember that there are ticklish and tender spots, too; don't be rough when you brush his flank, for example, or around his face and head. And never use a currycomb on his face or his lower legs or on any spot where the bones aren't well padded with flesh. It would feel about the same if somebody tried to comb your hair with a garden rake.

Even after a hard, thorough brushing (especially in the winter, when a horse doesn't look any better when you get through than he did when you started), there will be loose hairs and dust and dander on the surface. That's one of the things you collected all those old towels for. A few swipes will finish him off nicely.

All of this should be done every day, and not just for the sake of cleanliness. It's also a very good way to keep track of your horse's condition and health. If you just see him long enough to throw some hay into his stall, say, in the winter, how do you know he isn't losing flesh under all that hair? If you don't clean his hooves frequently, how can you be sure he isn't picking up a case of thrush? You have to feel his sides as you brush him, and get your nose right down there in his hoof. You'd be surprised at some of the things you notice while you're grooming. It's the same with a car: you don't notice all those tiny rust spots until you get down on your hands and knees to wax it. So grooming is a health checkup, too. Any additional work, like bathing, trimming whiskers, et cetera, can be done as it's needed and as you feel like it. But groom him every day. He won't *die* if you don't, probably; but if he's used to it, he'll be bitterly disappointed!

The third thing that will make your chores easier, along with the right attitude and having a regular, come-what-may routine, is having all your supplies handy. You remember we talked about this when we discussed building a barn and storage space. When you get your horse, you'll see what I mean. If you're able to have a barn with everything under one roof and a hayloft overhead, your chores will be relatively simple. Do whatever has to be done about the water, depending on what time of the year it is. Run upstairs (being sure you shut the stall door behind you!) and pick up a flake or two or three of hay, and throw them either over the edge of the loft or down the hay drop into the stall. Run over to the grain can, scoop out breakfast, run back, and shoot *that* down into the grain dish. Run back downstairs, check around again that everything is as it should be (I walked into my neighbor's little barn one day to find his mare sloshing around in her stall because he'd been in such a hurry that morning he forgot to turn off the water faucet!), and you're through with morning chores. See how great it is to have everything stored right where you want it?

To do your chores right, you also need the right kind of materials to work with, in sufficient amounts. Hay, grain and bedding. I don't know if your horse will be lucky enough to have a good pasture to graze in in the summer or not, so I can't even estimate what he'll need for hay and grain then. Anyway, in the summer it's easy to go get more. So let's figure out a good winter's supply—six months' worth—plus a little allowance for an early winter, a late spring, or a gluttonous 1,200-pound horse.

Some people will tell you that you can figure out how much hay your horse should have daily, to the ounce, by his body weight. I don't see how they do it. I know some great big horses that get potty on very little hay; and Mark, who couldn't possibly have weighed over 1,000 pounds, *never* got enough hay. I kept giving him more, and more, until that little thing was eating nearly a whole bale a day—in the winter, without doing a lick of work—and he still polished it all off in about half an hour—not a single seed left—and he never got a hay belly at all.

So start in feeding what most people think is a reasonable amount of hay for a horse that size, and then see what happens. For almost any horse, though, 150 good-sized bales should get you through the winter, with some left over.

The quality of the hay is extremely important. It should look and smell good to *you*. Really nice hay smells *delicious*. It should have a greenish cast (but should not *be* "green") and should contain clover or alfalfa as well as timothy. Again—time to call in your expert, as this is too important to make a mistake about. Hay is expensive these days, but good hay doesn't cost a lot more than bad hay. Never feed your horse as much as a mouthful of hay that looks or smells moldy or musty! Check it over every time you pick it up, because moldy hay is lethal to a horse.

Grain can and probably should be brought in by the bag, a hundred pounds or so at a time. You can always use a sled in the winter to haul it from the driveway to the barn, and in small amounts like this you can easily keep it in a mouseproof container. Most people still like to feed oats. They should be crushed or crimped rather than whole, because it's thought that a horse is able to get more nourishment from them in that form with less waste. Many barns feed a little corn in the winter as a side dish, since it's said to be "heatening." Horses dearly love to gnaw corn off the cob, anyway, and then play with the cobs. And you should add a little bran to the oats, too. It's good for the horse's coat, and it helps keep him from being constipated, especially when he isn't getting enough exercise. About a spoonful a day should be plenty. (Don't overdo the bran, for pretty obvious reasons!)

Or you can buy bags of feed mix put out by your local feed dealer or one of the national companies. Some of this is called sweet feed because it has molasses in it. There are several kinds of pellets on the market now, too; some are meant to take the place of grain, and some are a substitute for hay. You can get a lot of opinions on all of this. One horseman will swear by sweet feed and another will swear at it. I fed Mark mostly oats, partly sweet feed, a little "conditioner," and a lot of hay. I think hay is better for a playful horse, anyway, than just some pellets in a bucket, because hay gives him something to do for a while. Besides, the smell of fresh hay—well, what kind of a barn would it be without it? But do what you and your experts think best.

You can't go too far wrong, though, with clean, high-quality oats, a little corn in the winter, a bit of bran, a block of mineralized salt, and good hay. Carrots are fine fodder, too, but cut them up and put them in with the grain. Horses relish a really astonishing variety of goodies, too, like bread and cookies and so on. So go ahead and treat him occasionally. Just always put any treats in his *dish,* and don't overdo it, or you'll wind up with a spoiled little kid who won't eat his vegetables until he gets his dessert.

Now that we've got him well fed, we have to figure on how to keep the "end products" of all that food from being a total disaster. Obviously you don't want your horse standing knee deep in manure, so a daily stall cleaning is necessary. Then, since you'll be taking out some bedding every time you clean—either because it's stuck to the manure or because it's wet—you'll have to replace it every few days.

With what? Sawdust, most likely—at least in this part of the country. I've heard that down South they sometimes use pine needles, or there may be some other absorbent material that happens to be cheap and in good supply where you live. Or you may want to use the baled commercial bedding made from sugar cane. It's supposed to be fire-resistant (which is certainly a huge plus), absorbent, and soft; and, being neatly baled, it's easy to bring in and store. But I've never tried it, so I can't tell you about it from firsthand experience. Maybe you know somebody who can. (It *sounds* good.)

The traditional stall bedding—straw—might be cheap enough where you live. Around here, though, when you can find it, it's even more expensive than hay, and entirely out of the question for most people. It may not be all that wonderful, anyway. It makes a very pretty stall, as long as the stall is clean, but it does make stall cleaning messy and difficult. I've even tried peat moss, buying up broken bales cheap in the fall, but it seemed to me that it was *too* absorbent. That happened to be a very wet November, and the peat moss sucked the moisture right out of the air, so that it was already damp when I put it in the stall. That can be a little depressing.

So sawdust may be *your* best bet, too. You might have to borrow a pickup truck, or the sawmill might deliver it to you. If you have a ten-by-five-foot bin filled up nearly to the ceiling in the fall, it should last through the winter. You have to remember not to be wasteful with it, though, or you'll need a whole barnful of sawdust. Don't throw it out by the forkful. Pick up the manure, and then shake the fork a little to let the clean bedding sift through—and remove only the wettest of the "wet spot." (Most horses will pretty regularly choose one place to urinate.) Then fluff the bedding around, mixing the damp with the dry. You don't want a bone-dry stall—it isn't good for your horse's hooves. By being careful and thrifty you can make a little bedding go a long way and still have a clean stall.

Fill your bin as late in the fall as possible, shoveling the bedding from the truck through the opening provided in the wall, which should be only as high as you can throw sawdust. The "door" of the bin inside, then, should have a panel at the bottom that will slide up and down. At first, when you slide this up, the sawdust will slide out. As the supply dwindles, you can open up the whole door and go right into the bin.

You'll begin to notice pretty soon that the manure pile out behind the barn seems to be growing. Don't despair. You might be so unlucky as to have to pay somebody to haul it away every month or so, but see first if you can find a cash buyer for it. Nurseries, farmers and mushroom growers, among others, might pay you handsomely for your pile, and even come and pick it up for you. Sometimes a simple ad in the local paper brings amazing results, attracting to your barn everyone from truck farmers to little old ladies with plastic bags. One man's trash is indeed another man's treasure.

Meanwhile, between pickups, there's no need to be embarrassed. Sprinkle some lime to keep down odor and flies and to add to the fertilizer value. And remember, it's organic, it's biodegradable, and it was manufactured without the use of petroleum products!

Chapter Seven: Doctoring... from the Ground Up

Once you're a horse owner, two of the most important men in your life (or, increasingly, women) will be the farrier and the veterinarian. I'm sure you know what a veterinarian is. "Farrier" is a word that comes from *ferrum,* the Latin word for iron. We've changed the spelling a little and also the meaning, as the farrier is no longer simply any ironworker or blacksmith but more specifically one who shoes horses. (A farrier may also be a general blacksmith, however.)

Some farriers have mastered the art of farriery to a greater degree than others. A really good farrier combines the virtues of extensive training (there are many schools for it), a willingness to keep on learning, a strong back, a lot of patience, and a real love for horses. If he doesn't have the last two, he won't stay in the business very long, because shoeing some horses can be a trying, wearying experience.

You should find and hire the best farrier available to you. Your friends at the barn will know who he is. He may not charge you a penny more than a less competent one, but even if he does, it's worth it. This is one area where false economy can really hurt.

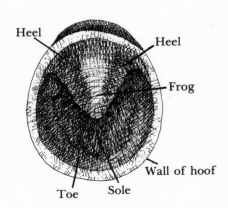

Heel   Heel   Frog   Wall of hoof   Toe   Sole

"No foot, no horse": truer words were never spoken. You can expect a little problem now and then, but a perpetually lame horse is a constant worry and expense and is virtually useless, especially if it's a gelding that can't even be sold for breeding when all else fails.

A horse's hoof is a complex, delicately balanced mechanism capable of supporting hundreds of pounds of weight and withstanding enormous impact. An ill-fitting shoe or improperly trimmed hooves can

61

You can see that even over a low jump, a horse's relatively small feet must be capable of withstanding the enormous impact when the combined weight of horse and rider hits the ground. (Photo by Dave Stark.)

upset this mechanism tremendously. Under natural conditions, the walls of the hoof will grow out at about the same rate as they wear down, and anything unusual about the horse's gait would be more or less compensated for in the wearing-down process.

But in a natural state, remember, horses just don't normally exert themselves all that much, or put undue strain on their feet. When we require a horse to "work," it needs shoes. A shoe, of course, acts as a buffer between the ground and the wall of the hoof and prevents the wall from wearing down—and that's where a lot of the trouble starts. Therefore, the farrier is called upon to take the place of nature by trimming off the hooves frequently and resetting the shoes. It sounds quite simple, and in most cases it is, but it can also be very complicated indeed.

Consider, for instance, all the corrective shoeing. Not all horses' legs are perfectly formed, and so not all horses walk and trot perfectly. They can toe in or toe out, wing, paddle, hit one foot with another, and, for all I know, waddle! So the farrier must be able to diagnose these imperfections and to correct them by carefully shaping the hooves and shoes. You may also want him to place a thick leather pad between the hoof and the shoe, especially in front, if you'll be riding where it's stony. Otherwise you may have to stop to pick out rocks every time your horse starts to hobble.

Some people—I, for one—like to have pads put on, anyway, because they'll keep out debris and prevent painful bruises. But the resilient center part of the bottom of a horse's foot, called the frog, is his principal shock absorber, and the pad prevents direct contact between the frog and the ground. So a resilient material of some sort must be inserted as compensation. The old favorite material, oakum and pine tar, is still very popular, although a new silicone has been favorably received. If your horse just naturally doesn't "grow foot" fast enough and his hooves are always too short, pads will help to keep him from being sore-footed all the time from stone bruises.

With or without pads, there's the question of shoes. My favorite farrier tells me that the racetracks have been experimenting with those nifty new plastic shoes that come in colors and are glued on, but he says that a lot of the trainers are going back to metal shoes, indicating that the plastic kind may not be working out too well. The metal shoe is punched

(LEFT) Before the farrier can reset your horse's shoes, he must pull the old ones off, clean the sole and frog very thoroughly, and trim the hooves. Here Don Wilfong is just starting to work on Shadow's forehoof. (Photo by James Dandelski, courtesy of Mrs. Joe Clark.) *(RIGHT) The hoof is clean now, the old shoes have been pulled, and Don Wilfong is carefully paring and shaping the wall of the hoof. A visit from the farrier needn't be dreaded if your horse has been taught to behave himself and stand patiently.* (Photo by James Dandelski, courtesy of Mrs. Joe Clark.)

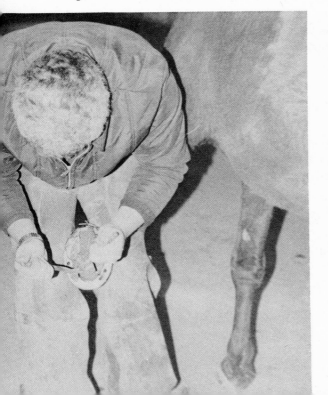 

with holes so it can be nailed onto the hoof. This looks terribly painful but is really only boring. A good farrier always fits the shoe to the hoof and not vice versa, no matter how many trips to the anvil this means or how much quicker it would be to snip off a little more hoof. He might even make his own shoes, in which case he'll undoubtedly have to charge you more. Most farriers use blanks of the proper size and heat them in order to shape them.

The average horse needs his shoes pulled, his hooves trimmed, and his shoes reset about every six or eight weeks. But horses vary a lot in this respect, even from one hoof to another! Mark's hind feet needed resetting almost every four weeks, because they grew fast and at too much of an angle, whereas I think I could have let his front ones go all winter, if I hadn't cared how long they got, as the angle remained perfect.

Depending on how you'll be using your horse, his ideal hoof length might be anywhere from three inches to as much as five, as on a three-gaited Saddle Horse. A good farrier will be able to tell you what's suitable and will trim them correctly. The angle of the hoof is even more important than the length, because the wrong angle can really lame your horse. Get a really good farrier who understands your kind of horse and trust him to know his business.

This goes for the type of shoe as well. See what he suggests. As a rule, ordinary plates will suffice for most pleasure horses, but there is a bewildering array of shapes designed for individual needs and problems. You might decide to "pull shoes" come fall for the duration of the winter (he'll still need trimming). Or, if you love cold-weather rides, you might decide instead to ask for barium calks to be put on the shoes to aid in traction on snow and ice. Some people also use pads in winter to keep the snow from balling up heavily in the hooves. Let your circumstances dictate.

Once you find a good farrier, you'll want to keep him by making his job as easy as possible. Clean your horse's hooves every day. This will help you avoid thrush, a nasty-smelling condition amounting more or less to "hoof rot"; or, if it happens anyway—since thrush can appear in the best of barns—you'll be able to spot it right away. If ever, in your daily cleaning, you notice a worse than usual odor or see and feel that the frog is getting black and "mushy," call the vet right away. He'll clean the hoof out thoroughly and will probably advise you to treat it with a copper sulfate medication or just plain chlorine bleach. In any case, you'll need his advice.

By cleaning the hooves daily, you'll get your horse accustomed to

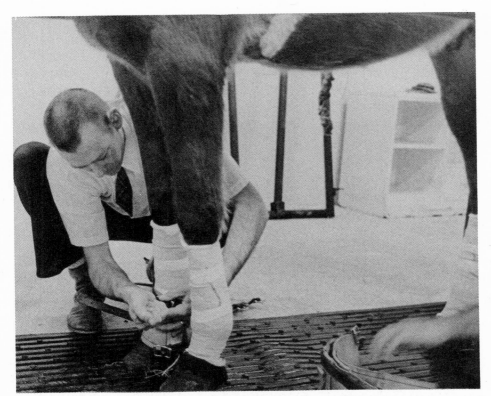

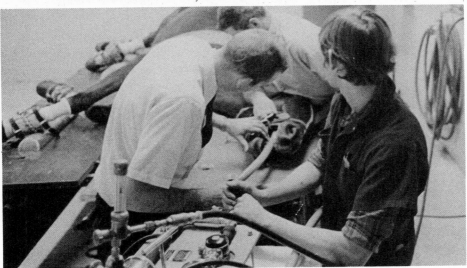

(TOP) This is a special kind of leg bandaging, since the horse is being prepared for surgery. However, it's also an excellent example of a good job. Any clips or pins you use must be well covered with tape, like this, or your horse can pull them out and injure himself. (BOTTOM) This is a frightening picture, but it's very reassuring, too. Nowadays, surgical procedures for animals are almost the same as for people, with monitors and other devices that reduce risk considerably. Here an oxygen tube is being inserted. (Photos by Richard Hallberg, courtesy of Moonbrook Veterinary Hospital.)

having his feet handled, and he'll behave himself for the farrier. Most farriers will put up with a lot in the way of bad-mannered "clients," but the better your horse behaves, the quicker things will go and the better your relationship will be with this very busy, very important person. I've seen shoeing jobs take anywhere from less than an hour on a pleasure horse to four hours on a gaited show horse or Walker, so your loved one had better be prepared to stand around on three legs, very patiently, for some time.

Under no circumstances present a farrier with a really bad-mannered horse. It just isn't fair. If persistent, gentle handling on your part doesn't seem to be improving the horse's manners—and if he *ever* offers to kick at you—call in your expert at once. If both his and your efforts fail, you'll have to consider getting rid of the horse. His hooves *must* be attended to, preferably without anyone having to take his life in his own hands to do it.

Your farrier will be extremely grateful if, between the two of you, you can decide what your horse's requirements will be and set up a regular schedule. It'll make his life a lot less complicated. You may still have to call him up between regular appointments for a pulled shoe or whatnot; he expects a few emergencies. But it is *not* an emergency when you've just put off or forgotten to call him till your horse is walking on his elbows and hocks. That's thoughtlessness and negligence.

Now, what about that other important fellow, the vet? He can be, after you, your horse's best friend. You had your horse vetted before you bought him. If you like that vet and like what you hear about him, he's a good choice. If not, try another one, but don't go shopping around too much. Your vet should be *your* friend, too, and it's better if he knows your horse's medical history at least from the time you bought him.

Horse doctoring is best left to horse doctors or to very experienced horsemen. So, especially at first, when all this is new to you, don't hesitate to call the vet if you even suspect something may be wrong. It's better to feel like a pest than to feel awful because you weren't a pest and something got a head start on you. The vet would rather catch something at the first sign of it, too. And as far as being a pest is concerned, and getting all excited about something really dumb, you wouldn't be the first person to do that. I remember calling my own expert once and reporting that I was finding some strange-looking "marbles" in my horse's hooves when I cleaned them. He came out with his corn knife, expecting to have to "operate," then laughed and told me the horse's hooves were just "shedding." I still don't exactly understand what that was all about, but evidently it's normal. So your vet won't mind a few false alarms if you don't cry wolf *too* often, and he'll appreciate your concern and awareness. It's people who don't notice, or don't care, who give him his worst headaches.

As with the farrier, you should try to schedule ahead with your vet for the routine work—the wormings and the usual inoculations.

And for everyone you call in to attend to your horse or give you advice—the vet, the farrier and your expert—have the horse ready, and be ready yourself. Nothing is more aggravating to a vet who is on a tight schedule than to arrive on time at a barn, and then be forced to waste priceless time because the horse is out in the pasture and playing coy about being caught. Also, keep in mind that many treatments require the assistance of at least a steady hand on the halter, and no vet should be expected even to give a shot without a responsible person on hand to help him.

So, how much does all this cost? Once again, I don't know. You can find out what the minimum will be, though, by calling a vet and asking what the shots and wormings will cost for a year, and by calling a farrier to get a fairly good idea what he charges. Then you just hope and pray that your horse doesn't get sick or lame or injured and keeps all his shoes on. These days, a sick or lame horse can be very expensive, indeed.

Although a good vet and a good farrier are very important, there's a lot that you yourself can do to keep your horse healthy, too. The right amounts of high-quality feed and plenty of clean water will go a long way. Sanitation is important, too, so wash out that vinyl grain dish often, and scrub the water bucket the same day. (Many horses like to dunk their hay; or they dribble grain into their water, which soon turns into a powerful-smelling gruel.) Feed the hay right on the stall floor, not from a manger. If he has to reach down to eat it, he's less likely to get dust and tiny seeds into his eyes. Besides, it's natural for a horse to reach to the ground for his fodder, and many horsemen feel that the closer you can stay to natural behavior, the better. Hay hung up high in a net may be cleaner, in that it won't be besmirched by dirty bedding, but it also rains dust downward into a horse's face as he tugs at it, and he'll be inhaling it. I don't like anything hanging in a stall that can get caught in a halter buckle, either.

Some horsemen feel that hay fed from the floor is too unsanitary, and that the horse will pick up worm eggs as he nibbles around. He probably will, but he'll be strewing hay about no matter where you put it originally and will be nibbling around anyway. A compromise might be a low manger, but then the horse would step into it and might hurt himself.

As to those little free-loaders, parasites—well, I asked my vet anxiously if my new horse might have some, and his reply was, "All horses have worms." It's a matter of degree, and what kind, and how dangerous they are. So a regular microscopic exam is in order (just take in a tiny bit of manure; a woman brought my vet a whole basketful once!), followed by worming when necessary. Most horses require a worming in the spring and one in the fall after the first frost, which will kill most of the eggs in the paddock.

Some varieties of intestinal parasites can do a lot of damage if given time. There's probably no way you can avoid them entirely, but by staying ahead of them you can easily make sure they're never a real threat to your horse's health. One sign of a heavy infestation is a horse eating well but doing poorly. Never let it get that far, though. A horse will sometimes consume great quantities of good feed and still lose flesh for another reason: his teeth need floating. This means that the sharp edges on his teeth need to be rasped down. Some horses have a lot of trouble with this, while others never seem to have any until they get quite old. Watch your horse eat his grain. If it dribbles out as he chews, that's a bad sign. Another sign is noticeable amounts of whole grain in the manure. A horse has to be able to do a pretty good job of chewing in order to get all the nourishment out of his food. Obviously, if the grain comes out looking the same as when it went in, something's wrong—and it's no wonder his ribs are starting to poke out. Stick your hand into his mouth, pull his tongue out of the way, and feel around, being *very* careful to keep your fingers pressed against the inside of the cheek and *not* where he could mistake one for a carrot and snip it off! You may be amazed at how razor-sharp the edges of some of those teeth are. Young horses with their new teeth coming in may have soreness, too, but that's usually only temporary.

A few farriers nowadays know how to float teeth, but most don't. Most vets probably know how, but a lot of them don't like to do it. If your vet can't or won't, you have to hunt around for a "specialist." I was watching one of these gentlemen recently at my favorite barn—everybody was getting his teeth checked—and it was really fascinating. Oddly enough, none of the horses seemed to mind at all, although they made some strange faces, and they all seemed to like the minty-smelling "mouthwash" that came afterward! I asked the fellow what his profession was called, and he said, "Some people like to call me an equine dentist, but I call myself a tooth floater." So much for fancy titles.

Many horses have one or more minor health problems that are easy to contend with and are no real threat with special care. I advised not to buy a horse that's heavey, but the condition is so common in older horses that you may have acquired one, if he suited you well in all other respects. Consult with your vet, of course, because the horse will need extra attention. Dust aggravates the problem, so the vet may advise you to feed a pelletized hay substitute; or maybe all you'll have to do is feed very clean hay and sprinkle it lightly with water to keep the dust down. A heavey horse should never be asked to do fast work. You couldn't game him, for instance. Many horses with only a minor wind ailment, though, are serving admirably as pleasure horses.

Or your horse may have dry hooves which need a little attention. A good dressing, applied with good judgment, will take care of them. Ask your expert to look at your horse's hooves and advise you how much dressing to use and how often. It's never a good idea to slop on great amounts of dressing every day. You could easily wind up with hooves that are too soft. And any horse with any foot problem requires an especially good farrier. In fact, he can advise you better than anyone else.

There are so many minor health problems that I couldn't possibly mention them all. But you can keep them to a minimum through continual observation. You take care of your horse every day. "Learn" him so well that you'll immediately notice anything unusual. *Notice* if he coughs or sneezes or has a runny nose or runny eyes. When you clean the stall, *notice* if his manure seems normal, too dry and hard, or too wet and soft. A firm but slightly moist manure is a sign that his innards are in good working order and that he's drinking enough water and getting enough salt and not too much bran. *Notice* if he's eating heartily or is going off his feed. Pay attention, in other words, to all these little signals that are the horse's only way of telling you what shape he's in.

You'll need to keep a cupboard stocked with some of the more frequently used dressings, infection fighters, and so on. Have a talk with your vet; he'll know what's best to keep on hand. Then always consult him before "doctoring" with anything—your diagnosis might be faulty! Every barn should have two first-aid kits—one for your horse and one for you. And every horse owner should be familiar with the contents and know how to use them properly. Always keep the vet's phone number handy, along with those of two or three other vets in case you can't reach yours and need one at once.

One of the most important things you can do to keep your horse healthy is to make sure he is cooled out properly. *Never* work him into a sweat and then go away and leave him standing there without a cooler, or, worse yet, with his nose in a bucket of water. Hot horses must be cooled out gradually and should never be given more than a small sip or

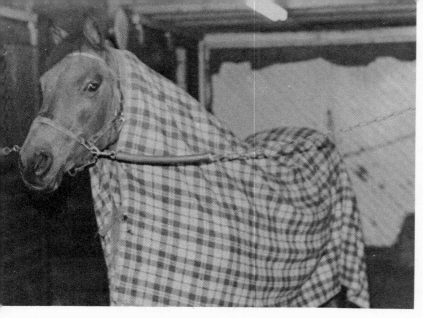

two of water until they are. If it's summer and he's only sweating mildly, put him into his stall or paddock without water for an hour or so. If he's really wet and overheated, you can walk him on a lead until he's mostly dry and then towel him off, or you can put a cooler on him and leave him cross-tied until he dries off by himself. (Cross-tied, because otherwise he'll pull at his cooler. You don't want him to get it down around his legs and scare himself silly.) How long this will take depends on how hot he was, the temperature of the air, and the humidity. In any case, he can't have water again until he's breathing normally and is bone dry.

Like everything else, it's harder in the winter. Even if he's been blanketed, his coat will be thicker, and he will sweat more with less exertion than he does in the summer. Moreover, it'll take a lot longer for him to dry off and cool out, with all that hair to contend with. It's also more difficult to tell whether he's really dry to the skin. Your best bet is not to work him to a frazzle in the winter in the first place. You can have a nice, long, leisurely ride in the frosty air without any worries, but a short *fast* one will mean hours of care when you get home. (Those of you who live in balmier climates don't have to worry about this sort of thing. Count your blessings.)

Remember that a horse may *die* if he's left to stand wet with sweat in the cold air, or allowed to drink his fill when he's overheated in *any* weather. Even feeding an overheated horse can be dangerous by causing colic. Colic is only gas on the stomach, but a horse can't burp. So this condition can be hideously painful for him, and in thrashing around in his pain, he can cause himself serious injury, not the least of which is "twisted gut." If you ever notice your horse in apparent discomfort, stall-walking, shifting his feet, pointing at his belly—or, of course, any signs at all of severe distress—call your vet at once! And always have colic medicine on hand, just in case the vet says to give your horse some while he's on his way.

Foundering, more accurately called laminitis, is also a possible result of letting your horse cool out too fast, watering too soon, or feeding heavily when hot. This is a crippling disease of the feet, often incurable and always extremely painful. Do your horse a big favor—and yourself, because you love him—and take great care that he's always properly cooled out.

If you're going to stable your horse at home, particularly in "suburbia," there's one more thing you need to be extremely aware of. Many of the ornamental shrubs and plants used extensively for landscaping are poisonous. The Japanese yew, for example, that's so very popular for landscaping, is also so very poisonous that many horses have died from nibbling on it. A mouthful can kill a horse in about five minutes, with no hope whatever of saving it. Even brown, dried, months-old clippings from these yew shrubs will kill in minutes!

You should find out—and remember—which plants are poisonous. (Go to the library, or ask your county extension service.) Then, just to be safe, never, never let anyone throw even grass clippings into your paddock or anywhere your horse could get at them. There may very well be bits of yew or other toxic plants mixed in with them—and even plain grass clippings can be toxic because they're green, and when piled up rather than spread to dry like hay grasses, they can very soon become moldy and lethal.

Another thing: *never* let your horse snack on *anything* when you're out riding. The most innocuous plants may have been sprayed with poisonous chemicals, for all you know. This is particularly apt to be true along a roadway, where defoliants are still sometimes used. Poison aside, it's never a good idea to let your horse eat with a bit in his mouth, anyway. There's always the chance that he might choke on a big mouthful; it makes a real mess of the bit; and he'll soon learn to pay attention to what there is to eat instead of to you, and you'll wind up having to haul his head off the ground at every other step.

So get that list of poisonous plants, check your paddock or pasture carefully, and then be very sure your horse has access to only the food he's supposed to have. Avoid a real tragedy.

If you do *your* best and let the farrier and the vet do *theirs*, your horse may very well stay hale and hearty as long as you own him. The expression "healthy as a horse" didn't come about for no reason at all, you know.

Chapter Eight:
Hunt, Stock or Saddle

You've probably realized by now that I don't consider riding a horse the most important part of owning one. And if you truly love the beasts, it really isn't. You'll find just as much enjoyment in the caring, and the companionship, as you will in the "equitating." However, riding the horse *is* the reason for getting ready, building, buying and owning. Theoretically, anyway, one buys a horse to have something to ride. And if you've had enough lessons by now, from a good teacher on a good horse, you should be ready to saddle up and have some fun.

In this country the three most popular styles of riding are hunt seat, saddle seat and stock seat. If you've already found your favorite learning stable (most of them specialize in one of the seats) and have purchased your horse and tack, you've already chosen the seat you'll be using. But if you're just reading this book for future reference, you may still be undecided.

Stock seat is "western," and stock saddles are "western" saddles. I'm sure you've at least seen them, and probably some of your horse-minded friends use them, because they're very popular, even among easterners. Any kind of saddle can be used for ordinary pleasure riding, but some are more appropriate for some kinds of horses than others, and even in a small horse show, each performance class requires its own kind of tack. A western pleasure class, for instance, or stock seat equitation, would require a stock saddle and a suitable bridle. So be careful about which style you choose for pleasure riding, in case you decide to show later on.

Every type of saddle was originally developed with a particular purpose in mind. A stock saddle was designed for working "stock"—cattle. The cowboy often rode his horse all day long, day after day, and fine riding form was the least of his worries. The high cantle and the general shape of the stock saddle allowed him to "slouch" comfortably, and it also gave him a little something to back him up when his horse climbed hills or made sudden jumps as it worked. The high, wide pommel of the stock saddle also gave him support, and its horn was

72

used as a "handle" to tie a rope to—maybe with a cow or calf or steer bucking around at the other end.

You, however, are not likely to be riding every day from dawn to sunset, nor are you likely to be working, let alone roping, cattle—and neither are most of your friends who ride stock seat. Why then is this seat so popular?

Well, there's a whole mystique surrounding western riding; it's a world of its own. People just *like* it; they like the way it makes them feel. They know they're not cowboys, that most of their horses wouldn't recognize a cow if they saw one. But nowadays, in spite of its practical, workaday beginnings, a majority of stock seat riding is either purely for pleasure or just as show-oriented as the so-called English seats.

Stock seat equitation rules are just as stringent as saddle seat or hunt seat at a show, and good riding form is very much required. An old-time cowboy would bust his vest laughing. But for modern times and modern tastes and uses, the stock horse as show horse is in high demand. The open western pleasure class is often the largest class in a show.

One of these big western pleasure classes will be likely to include a great many quarter horses, many Appaloosas, some Arabians and Morgans, a Saddlebred or two, many grade horses (not purebred), and some ponies for the youngest riders. Three gaits are called for: a flat-footed walk, a jog (slow trot), and a lope.

There are also western pleasure breed classes, and the requirements

Picking up her ribbon at a 4-H show is this stock seat rider. Note the simple curb bit and the light, but not loose, *rein. A western suit and hat like this are proper for stock seat classes.* (Photo by Dave Stark.)

A hunt seat saddle is often accompanied by a full cheek snaffle bit like this one, which prevents the mouthpiece from being pulled sidewise through the mouth. King of the Rikers' *rider is perfectly outfitted in hunt seat attire.* (Photo courtesy of the American Quarter Horse Association, Amarillo, Texas.)

will vary somewhat from breed to breed. In an Arabian western pleasure class, for instance, the gaits called for would be the flat walk, jog-trot, lope and hand gallop. These variations simply take into consideration the breed's most valued gaits. In all western pleasure classes, though, stock seat saddles and bridles are mandatory, and the horses must go easily on a light (not "loose") rein. They are judged on manners, a smooth performance, substance and conformation.

If you choose stock seat for your everyday backyard riding, then, whether your horse is registered or grade, you'll be able to show him if you want to. If all your friends ride western, all the local clubs and shows are western-oriented, and you have no overwhelming desire to ride some other way, then western would probably be a wise choice. Quarter horses and Appaloosas are the most logical breeds to think of first for stock seat, but any horse that's trained for one-handed western riding and goes well that way would be just fine.

Hunt seat is also very popular in the United States, and it's what most people mean when they say "English." It's what they should mean, anyway, because this style originated in England and western Europe and is still practically the only way they ride over there, other than dressage, or "high school" riding. Fundamentally, hunt seat can be either balanced seat or forward seat riding, with appropriate saddles for each. They range from park saddles with nearly straight cut flaps and not much dip in the seat, to strictly forward seat jumping saddles with a very deep seat and flaps that extend well forward and are equipped with thick knee rolls to aid the rider when jumping.

Again, there is a purpose for every type of saddle. For work on the flat and the occasional low jump, a park saddle is probably indicated. For

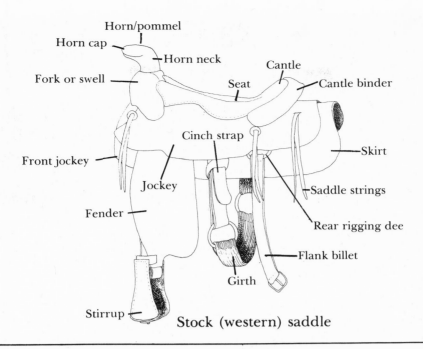

Stock (western) saddle

Horn/pommel
Horn cap
Horn neck
Fork or swell
Cantle
Seat
Cantle binder
Front jockey
Cinch strap
Jockey
Skirt
Fender
Saddle strings
Rear rigging dee
Flank billet
Girth
Stirrup

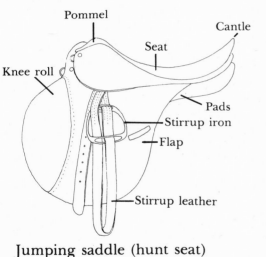

Jumping saddle (hunt seat)

Pommel
Seat
Cantle
Knee roll
Pads
Stirrup iron
Flap
Stirrup leather

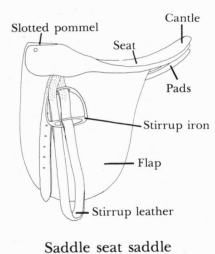

Saddle seat saddle

Slotted pommel
Seat
Cantle
Pads
Stirrup iron
Flap
Stirrup leather

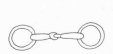

Hunting
snaffle bit

Copper mouth
curb bit

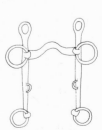

Loose ring
Pelham bit

extensive, advanced jumping, you should definitely have the added advantages of the forward seat saddle. As with stock saddles, there's a wide variety of designs to choose from. The important thing with any tack is that it suits your purpose and is comfortable for both you and your horse.

There is also a wide variety of bridles and bits for both stock and hunt seat. Some are very simple, and some are so specialized in purpose as to seem quite bizarre to anyone lucky enough not to need them. Most western horses are ridden on a simple curb bit or a hackamore (a bridle with no bit in the mouth), although hackamores are usually forbidden in western equitation classes and are banned from some pleasure classes. And, generally speaking, a hunt seat saddle is accompanied by a snaffle or a Pelham bridle.

A curb bit works on the principle of applying leverage. You know what a lever does—it works on a fulcrum somewhere along its length that allows you to apply more pressure while expending less energy. If you want to pick up one end of a heavy board, say, you may have to expend quite a lot of energy to bend down and lift it up. But if the board is lying across a fulcrum, such as a log, it requires very little pressure applied to one end to raise the other end.

With a curb bit, the horse's mouth is the fulcrum, and the cheek or shank of the bit—the long side piece—is the lever. A ring at the top of each cheek, slightly above and slightly behind the mouth corner, to which the headstall of the bridle is attached, is one end of the lever. A ring at the bottom of the cheek, to which the rein is attached, becomes the other end. There's also a strap or chain running from top ring to top ring under the horse's jaw. Therefore, when your hands pull back on the reins, the combination of the bit being firmly fastened to the headstall and firmly fastened to the curb strap or chain results in your pulling against not only his mouth but also his lower jaw. Some people think that for this reason a curb bit is cruel. It certainly can be, in the wrong hands, but so can any other bit, or a hackamore, in the wrong hands. If you use a curb, you have to remember that you may be exerting more pressure than you realize, and ride accordingly. A well-trained horse with a good mouth shouldn't need a curb to control him, but most western horse show classes require them.

A snaffle bit works on an entirely different principle. It's a straight bar, either solid, or jointed in the middle (in which case it's a jointed snaffle), that rests somewhat higher in the horse's mouth than a curb, and there is no lever action at all. There's only one ring at each end of the bar or "mouth" of the bit, and no chain running underneath. When you pull on the reins, you're simply pulling against the corners of the horse's mouth. While a snaffle is thought of as a soft bit, for use with light-mouthed horses, and a curb as a severe bit, in either case it's much more a matter of training and of how you use it. No horse trained by a good trainer has a hard mouth, because good trainers simply don't let it happen. A hard mouth is caused by incompetent riders. Every horse is born with a soft mouth, but if he is forced to develop hardness in self-defense, he will. Since this is another thing your expert will have checked out ahead of time, your horse shouldn't have such a hard mouth that he requires a grotesque bit plus a ham-fisted, 200-pound rider to stop him. (If he does, you have my sympathy; but there's hope, with retraining and better riding.)

A Pelham bit, another popular choice for hunt seat riders, also provides a variety of mouthpieces and lengths of cheek, but basically it's a combination of curb and snaffle, all in one bit. There are rings at the ends of the bar, as with a snaffle, plus attached cheeks and a curb strap or chain. One set of reins is attached to the snaffle rings and becomes the snaffle rein, while another, thinner set is fastened to the cheeks and becomes the curb rein. Curb, snaffle and Pelham bits all require the right kind of bridle to go with them.

The full bridle is also called a double bridle, or sometimes a Weymouth bridle. At a horse show, three-gaited and five-gaited

A full bridle is complex, and the details are usually hard to see in a photo. So here Chocolate Royale gives us a good close look at hers. You can see how the two bits fit into the mouth, with the snaffle well behind the curb. (Photo by James Dandelski, courtesy of Holliday Farm.)

Saddlebreds are always shown in a full bridle. Morgan and Arabian park horses and most saddle seat pleasure horses usually wear full bridles, too, although other bitting may be permitted. As you might guess from the word "double," two separate bits are used: a light snaffle with small rings (called a bradoon), and a fine, light, fairly long cheeked curb. This may seem like quite a mouthful for a horse, but the snaffle, or bradoon, is placed behind the curb so that it fits properly against the corners of the mouth, and the curb is in front of and slightly lower than that.

One of the most common misconceptions among beginners is that, in a full bridle, the snaffle is for steering and the curb for stopping. This does *sound* logical, but it's entirely off the track. With the curb and the snaffle rein attached to entirely separate bits, a lot more flexibility and sensitivity are possible than with both reins attached to one bit. With the Saddlebred and park-type show horses, the head-set is of vital importance, not only for appearance's sake, but also because a great deal of animation—what you might call "high stepping"—is demanded. The set of the head greatly influences this by shifting the horse's center of balance slightly to the rear. This, in turn, makes the horse lighter in front and enables him to achieve the desired motion more easily.

So a full bridle is used to get that proper head-set. The snaffle has a tendency to raise the head; whereas the curb, once the head is raised, tends to bring the horse's muzzle back, resulting—with training, good riding, and the right conformation—in a high but well-flexed head-set. Very little pressure—perhaps only a crooking of the little fingers—is needed, then, to produce subtle changes, because the horse is so extremely collected and so lightly held. Proper use of a full bridle demands a well-trained or willing-to-learn horse, good hands, and plenty of practice.

Talking about full bridles brings us to the third popular seat, saddle seat, also called "English" by many people; which is all right if you just want to distinguish it from "western," but saddle seat is virtually unknown in England. Oddly enough, some of the very best makers of saddle seat saddles *are* in England, but the style originated here. Or maybe it would be more truthful and accurate to say that it *survived* here, because it or something very similar to it can be seen in ancient carvings. And it's likely that it was once used in England, back when pacers were popular there as riding horses.

Somewhere along in the 1600s, though, someone in England noticed that the post-boys—the chaps who rode along on carriage horses as a control factor and status symbol (they wore gorgeous "liveries")—had very cleverly invented a new way to ride the trot. They "skipped a beat," sitting down only on every other stride. I'm sure they were destined to think of it sooner or later, since a stylish carriage horse had an equally stylish, rough trot. And, since trotting is a prettier, more impressive looking gait than pacing, it became fashionable to ride trotters soon after "posting" was invented to make it less painful as well. Pacers became so unloved, eventually, that the few that were left were sent over to the colonies.

Posting, or rising to the trot, brought about quite a drastic change in riding. Shorter stirrup leathers are required, because if the leathers are so long that the rider can't rise out of the saddle, he can't post, either. Then, when the stirrups are raised, resulting in a more acute angle of the knees, it's also more natural to lean just a bit forward, a combination which was soon seen to be much better, and safer, for jumping obstacles than the old foxhunter's "feet in the dashboard" method. Thus was born the forward seat.

Meanwhile, back in the colonies, New York City park riders and other fashionable eastern types picked up this new way of riding, too. But for a long, long time the southern and western ("western" meaning as far west as Kentucky, say, in those days) riders would have none of it. And they had an excellent reason for being so stubborn: for the most part, their horses did not trot. Therefore, there was no reason in the world for them to post, or to raise their stirrups so they *could* post. What they did have were saddle-gaited horses which, by breeding (remember all those rejected pacers) and with very little if any encouragement, could execute several smooth, ground-eating, four-beat gaits.

Why the difference? During this time, "up North," roads were already being built that were good enough to take vehicular traffic, and so trotters were coming into favor not only as saddlers but as harness horses. The old favorites, the easy-gaited pacers, were again becoming unfashionable.

But down South and out West, roads were still primitive, and riding was still more common than driving. When you went anywhere, you were apt to do it on the back of a horse. And since this could well mean being in the saddle many long days, the smoother the trip, the better. These four-beat, single-footing saddle gaits were so smooth and so relatively effortless that both horse and rider could reach their destination without being in the least exhausted.

The original saddle-gaited horses soon turned into our modern-day Saddlebreds and Tennessee Walkers. Both have pacing ancestors. And the saddle seat (now you can see where the term comes from—saddle-gaited) has survived right along with them. The only real change came

Randi Wightman riding Summer Melody—saddle seat, of course. Her saddle suit is the correct formal one for nighttime shows, worn with a man's shirt and tie and a derby. (Photo by Jamie Donaldson, courtesy of Saddle and Bridle)

about because nowadays we like our Saddlebreds (not our Walkers) to trot stylishly as well as do the other gaits, so we have shortened our stirrups just enough to make posting easy, without going to the extreme shortness of jumping length. Walking Horse riders still wear their leathers as long as they can reach them, because they never have to post.

Now, just as the forward seat is designed primarily for jumping and the stock seat for working cattle, the saddle seat is designed for its own particular purposes. The straight-cut flaps are suitable for the longer stirrups, and since there's no need for knee rolls, the flaps lie very close to the horse. The shallow seat also sits down very close to the horse's back, and the cutback pommel, with a wide slot at the front of the saddle, makes it fit down even more closely and allows for the typical Saddlebred or Walker's low, wide withers and high head-set. The result of all this is that the saddle seat saddle is perfectly designed for what is now its primary purpose—putting the rider where the horse can work best, by lightening the front; and, by being so close to the horse and unobtrusive, showing off the horse's conformation, which is important in saddle classes.

As with the other two seats, you'll find many horse show classes for saddle seat. Most of them will also require a full bridle; an exception is Walking Horse classes, which require a special, long-cheeked "Walking Horse bit."

All too often, horse people ride only one way—period! They don't even consider riding any other way, and sometimes they're even so narrow-minded they feel that any other way is wrong. I'm sure you've run across this kind of attitude already.

So I will have done a great deal here if I succeed only in convincing you that there is more than one "right" way to ride . . . and if I've actually persuaded you to branch out and learn to ride two or three different seats, then I certainly couldn't be happier! You're too young to put those blinkers on yet—get out and explore!

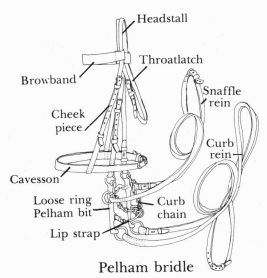

Western bridle with ear piece

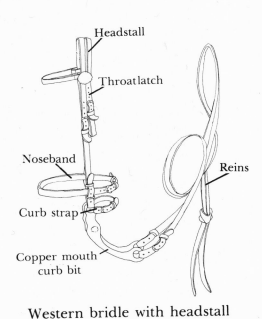

Western bridle with headstall

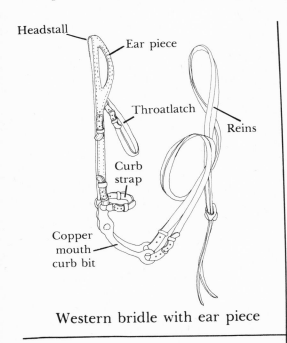

Pelham bridle

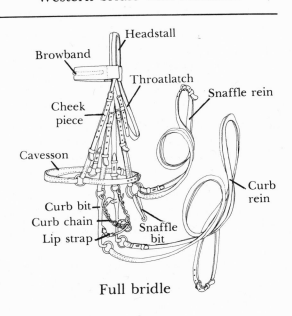

Full bridle

Chapter Nine: Finally— Riding and Showing

First of all, I'm not going to tell you how to ride a horse stock seat, saddle seat, hunt seat, or bareback. I couldn't, even if I were qualified (I'm not) and wanted to (I don't). To learn to ride, you need more than somebody telling you how it's done, and a few pictures. Books and magazines will be extremely helpful to you, but only as a backup. You need somebody to show you as well as tell you and to answer all your questions as you go along. Then you need to do it, by the hour, preferably under qualified supervision. This is the only safe, effective, reasonably fast way to learn to ride that I'm aware of. You can, however, with books, advice from knowledgeable friends, and an accommodating horse, teach yourself a great deal. It just isn't as safe, though, and it'll probably take you a lot longer to make any progress, what with the inevitable trial-and-error.

In any case, and with any seat, there are some fundamental things you can learn between lessons or on your own. Any time spent observing your horse closely will be well spent, for instance. Watch him while he's in the paddock. Study his anatomy; note how he moves that big body around. Exactly what's involved in a sudden turn—what muscles, and what shifts of weight? See how his head and neck are his "balancer"? And then imagine yourself on his back. What actions and weight shifts of your own would help or hinder him in his natural movements? The more time you spend hanging over the fence, observing—and understanding what you observe—the more intelligently you will ride.

All riding, as the old saying goes, is a matter of "keeping a leg on each side and your mind in the middle." Ninety percent of true horsemanship is in the mind. An equitation student may look just splendid on a horse—her form may be perfect—but unless she rides with intelligence she's only a rider, not a horseman. Most good equitation riders are also horsemen, but there are some who can really ride only one horse—and one that's pushbutton trained, at that. That's why many judges will ask the riders to change horses. You'll want to be able to ride any adequately trained horse well.

Even when the snow is too deep to do much riding, you can always bundle up, find a warm spot along the fence, and just visit and watch. You'll learn a lot about horses that way, if you really pay attention. (Photo by John Dandelski, courtesy of Edward Martin, D.V.M.)

To do that you have to think. And you have to get at least a general idea of how your horse feels. Again—observe him. Hang over the fence some more and find out how he feels about various things in his environment, and how he reacts to them. Other than food, of course, what things arouse his interest? How does he show that interest? What things frighten him, and how much, and what does he do when he's frightened? If an ambulance goes screaming past his paddock, does he raise his head, still chewing grass and only mildly alarmed, or does he turn inside out in panic? Enough of this kind of observation will give you a very good idea of how to handle him when you're riding and something unexpected comes up.

Let's say that you're riding along someday, the two of you, minding your own business, and suddenly his ears swivel around, his eyes get huge, he snorts and comes to a dead halt. What (you would be wise to wonder) does this *mean?* If you've watched him enough, you'll have at least some idea of whether it means, "Well, would you look at that!" and he's about to go on walking quietly along; or whether he's telling you, "I don't know about you, but I'm getting out of here!" and he's about to try to do just that. This is a very useful thing to know!

Riding is a partnership venture, after all. A horse is trained to understand what a rider is saying with her hands, legs and weight; so as long as you do it right, he'll probably know what you're trying to communicate. But since he's your partner, it's up to you to understand his language, too. There's no way that you can ride really well if your two-way communication system isn't in good working order. Your instructor and your school horse will teach you basic horse language, but your own horse will have his own feelings and his own ways of

An August afternoon, a woodland trail, and time to dream. Horse shows are fun and exciting, but to many people a long, leisurely ride with a fine horse for company is much more enjoyable. (Photo by Joan S. Byrne, courtesy of the American Saddle Horse Breeders Association.)

expressing those feelings. You will, too, and you may express yourself entirely differently from his previous riders, so allow yourselves some time to come to a perfect understanding, and put some effort into it.

Another fundamental part of any kind of riding is getting on and getting off. There are variations on the niceties of these maneuvers, but basically it's a matter of doing it safely and with a certain amount of grace. Mounting and dismounting constitute the two times when a rider's situation is the most precarious. He isn't really "on" yet, and settled into his saddle, but he's involved with the horse to the extent that an untoward movement of the horse affects him directly. Therefore, aim for a quick, graceful movement that cuts down on the length of time you're partially airborne!

Mounting a tall horse can be a problem. For me it can be a *real* problem. For one thing, since I am so short, my stirrup leathers are, too, of course. This means that if my horse is 16 hands high, I'm presented with a stirrup iron that comes to about my chin. And that agile I'm not. I usually manage, but it's hardly what anyone would call a graceful performance, since it consists mostly of a lot of puffing just to get my foot *up* that high, followed by more heavy breathing while I practically crawl up hand over hand and—at last—get my leg over the horse.

There are ways to avoid making this kind of spectacle of yourself, however. One way that is employed a lot by riders of hunters and jumpers, which are often tall animals, is simply to "get a leg up"—have a friend give you a helping hand or two. Another is equally simple: stand the horse next to a bale of hay and use the hay as a mounting block. Yet another is to "cheat" by lowering the near stirrup two or three holes, and then correcting it when you're on.

Whatever method you use, try to *spring* up off that right leg, and make it quick so as to be astride as soon as possible. Also, always have the reins in your left hand while you're mounting or dismounting, so as to retain some control if the horse should try to step out on you. And *never* let yourself slam down on his back. If you do, you'll hurt him, and if you do it very many times, he'll dread the ordeal so much that soon he'll be almost impossible to mount.

Even a beginner's awkwardness is no excuse for thudding down on a horse. No matter how out of balance you feel, if you feel yourself dropping heavily onto him, simply grab with your knees. This will break your fall ("stop your drop"), and then you can lower your weight onto the saddle gently. Your horse will certainly appreciate it, and you'll appreciate his continued good mounting manners.

If he's already been dropped on a few times, or he's just one of those horses that's eager to get on with it, he may need some training to make him hold still for a minute. Meanwhile, if he'll park out for you, that will often do the trick. A well-trained horse knows he isn't supposed to move around when he's been parked out. Besides, if he's tall, this will actually lower his back a smidge—maybe just enough to make the difference for you.

Practice until you *can* mount your horse by yourself. It's wonderful if someone will help you at home by holding him or giving you a leg up—or if you can make it from a bale of hay or a fence—but what if you're out on the trail alone sometime and have to get off to remove a stone from his hoof? And there isn't even a good-sized rock around? You don't have to worry about being graceful, in this situation, just as long as you can get up there; main strength and awkwardness will do just fine.

Also basic to any kind of riding is the awareness that your horse is "between hands and legs." Your legs can be used to help turn a horse, too, but for the moment let's say that your legs are used primarily to propel him forward, while your hands on the reins are restraining—they hold him back. Your teacher will have much more to say about this, but if you keep in mind that your horse's speed and degree of collection are mostly dependent on these two things, it may help you understand what your teacher is driving at.

A horse may be nine feet long from nose to tail and weigh 1,000 pounds. But remember that about half that length and about two-thirds of that weight are in front of the girth—between your hands (the bit, really) and your legs. A thorough understanding of this will go a long way toward making you a rider. It wouldn't do any harm at all just to sit and think about that now and then.

How about riding in the company of others, either along a woodsy back road or in the show ring? This requires a set of rules all its own, but again, it's basically a matter of common sense and consideration for others. A person riding in a group or in a show class who doesn't have any common sense or consideration can be anything from a nuisance to a menace. Try to avoid riders like that, and don't be one yourself. A little bit of group riding will show you what kind of behavior is likely to cause somebody some trouble.

Horses are herd animals, after all, and often it's a case of monkey see, monkey do. Your own horse, naturally, won't do anything you haven't asked him to do (well, usually!), but how about that little girl's pony? How accomplished a rider is the girl? Are you sure that if you decide to gallop on ahead a bit, her pony won't follow suit and scare her half to death or make her fall? Think, in other words, before you act.

In most groups of friends and neighbors, at least some of the horses are sure to be poorly trained, and you're lucky if one of them isn't downright uncontrollable. So be careful. Be a little choosey about the people you ride with, and the horses they're mounted on. All it takes is one show-off or one bad-mannered horse to create a really serious accident.

Another basic aspect of cross-country riding is knowing where to ride. It's odd how some people who wouldn't dream of trespassing on private property on foot will get on a horse or a snowmobile or a motorcycle and just set about trespassing in all different directions. Property owners can have lots of perfectly good reasons for not welcoming you and your horse, and whether those reasons seem good to you or not, the fact remains that they do own the property and have every right in the world not to want you. Before you let your horse set a hoof down in somebody else's woods or fields, ask for permission. They might be so pleased that you had the good manners to ask that they'll let you. If so, they'll probably let you keep the privilege as long as you respect it and show some responsibility. The first time you galumph gaily across a soft, seeded field—or, most sinful of all, leave a gate open—you can expect to be asked not to come back. If that gate let about sixty valuable cows scatter far and wide, you can expect, and deserve, a lot worse than *that*.

If all goes well with your riding, after a while you may get the urge to enter a local horse show. Perhaps you've joined a club that sponsors them. Remember your riding manners here, too, plus some manners about showing in particular. Again, some time spent in quiet observation at a few shows beforehand will give you an indication of what kinds of behavior are acceptable and what kinds are not.

A horse show is a chance to show off your horse, not yourself. In the first place, a show-off is seldom an endearing person; and in the second place, an exhibitionist stunt is potentially dangerous when pulled at a show because of the close proximity of so many people and horses. Try to be sensible, and somewhat humble. You'll make a lot of friends that way.

Since showing can be a big part of your riding fun, a few more words on the subject may not be amiss. You'll want your horse to behave and perform at a show at least as well as he does at home. Many horses are "hams" and do even better, and if you've bought a retired show horse you shouldn't have any problems. But what if your horse has always been a backyard pet and this is his first show? Even if he's used to being ridden in a group, he might suffer from a mild case of stage fright. Just think of all those people and all the noise they make, and all those lights, if it's at night. Your horse might not even like the looks of the show ring, the grandstand and the judges' box—not to mention the sound of the music, if there is any. I remember watching one thoroughly schooled young mare at her first horse show. She astonished all her friends by executing her figure-eight at a lively buck instead of a canter.

Well, the only way to get him used to shows is to show him. But you can make it easier for him by making things as familiar as possible. Get to the show grounds well head of your class time so he can get used to the surroundings. Give him time to rest up. Trailering can be very wearying for a horse who isn't an old hand at it. Lead him around and give him a long, close, unhurried look at the ring. And here's something most people don't think about at all: well before the show, handle and ride him wearing the clothes you'll be wearing in the ring. Horses are extremely sensitive to new smells, and the smell of your brand-new or just dry-cleaned outfit may only add to his worries. This also applies to new tack. Don't save up a saddle or a bridle just for show and spring it on him at the last minute.

To a horse, familiarity means security. So by all means try to make him feel at home, even when he isn't. If he has a favorite toy hanging in his stall at home, bring it along. Another horse of my acquaintance trained very well, but at his first show he fretted the whole time and refused to eat. It was a three-day show, and he actually lost weight. Upon returning home, he rushed into his stall and immediately hurried over to nudge his beloved toy, a plastic bottle hanging from a rope. He was just plain homesick. The next time he goes, I'm sure his "security blanket"—the plastic bottle—will go with him.

If you're half as smart as I think you are, and have some help, you won't have any great amount of trouble learning to ride. Mind your manners . . . don't let the horse forget about minding his . . . and have a great time.

Chapter Ten: Staying Out of Trouble

No matter how careful you are, sooner or later you'll probably get into trouble of some kind with your horse. If you do, try not to let it devastate you, because you're in good company. Even "my" barn, where everyone is wise in the ways of horses and very safety-conscious about handling them, some pretty peculiar, totally unexpected things happen now and again. And, yes, people get hurt occasionally.

In just one recent winter: I fell off a horse for the first time in my adult life, painfully readjusting my tailbone. An acquaintance had a horse jump onto her foot and smash it. Another woman was holding a big colt for his first haircut, and he panicked at the clippers and "hugged" her, bumping those hard, sharp hooves down both sides of her entire body. Another young lady had a horse slip on a snowy hillside, fall with her, and break her leg with not one but two forehooves. And my friend who's trained horses for probably forty years and hadn't been dumped for at least twenty fell off and broke three ribs.

All of this isn't meant to persuade you to take your new horse to the nearest auction barn. It's just to assure you that these things happen and that life still goes on. When I was your age and cadging occasional rides from kindly horse owners, I got hurt all the time. My injuries ranged from a stiff neck from executing a perfect somersault off a stumbling horse, through many, many pinched fingers, to getting bitten, kicked and—continually, it seemed—just plain stepped on. How many times I've had to hop around on one foot—after I'd finally gotten the other one out from under the horse!

And I can still remember how I felt about it. I was embarrassed, and I was afraid that if my aunt or the owner of the horse found out, it would be the end of my riding career. And maybe it would've been, but I never told a soul! (Actually, now that I'm a grown-up, too, I wish I *had* told someone—I would probably have received some sympathy and encouragement!) Well, why did I persist, even when it became apparent that I was hopelessly clumsy and accident-prone? For the same reason you would: I loved horses. "Until death do us part" was my attitude, I guess, and I did seem to be aiming in that direction sometimes.

I probably wasn't really so much accident-prone as I was ignorant. I just never had anybody around to show me how to handle horses safely. That's why I hope you will learn, if only to save yourself from all that battering.

Very few horses are really mean, and if your expert was worth his salt, you don't own a mean horse. But he is large, compared to you. He might easily weigh half a ton—to your measley little hundred pounds or so. And no matter how sweet-natured and calm he is, something, somewhere, someday is going to startle him. You can never predict what this might be, or when it's going to happen. He might say ho-hum to a backfiring truck rattling by with a flapping canvas, and then panic at a glimpse of a mouse running along a rafter. Then, too, even the most lethargic beast has his day every once in a while, when he's been stalled too long, or just because the sun has finally come out. He'll be "feelin' good" and surprise you with some unexpected high jinks.

So, while nobody wants you to be scared of your horse, and a certain number of bumps are inevitable, you can learn—at your friends' stable—how to avoid some of the bruises, for both you and your horse. A few hints are offered here, gleaned from my own black-and-blue-marked trail and that of some of my friends.

Check your horse, your tack, all your equipment and the environment constantly. This should become second nature to you. Horses do seem to have a marked suicidal bent sometimes. For instance, if you used any nails in the construction of your stall, check daily for loosened–up boards and nails sticking out. Check his halter. Check his shoes. Check the paddock for stray trash and remove it. Several times a day, check any heater or heater tape you're using. Check doors and hinges. Check screens. Check!

And never handle your horse too casually. Speak to him before you touch him. Horses are half asleep half the time. (Really! They rarely sleep soundly, the way we do.) So be sure he knows you're there before you slap him on the rump. Otherwise, he might just flinch lightly, or he might give you a demonstration of automatic reflexes that will put you on your ear.

I'll assume that your horse wouldn't deliberately kick at you, but he will kick at flies on his legs and his belly. Don't stand where a suddenly lifted front or rear hoof will catch you in the kneecap. When you're brushing with one hand, it's a good idea to rest the other on the horse, and when you go around behind him, make sure he feels your

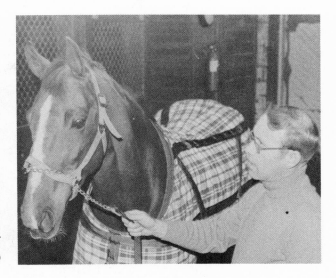

This shows clearly how a lead shank can be fastened to a halter to give the handler more "muscle" if it's needed. Otherwise, a horse can lift you right off your feet and not even notice you're dangling there. (Photo by James Dandelski, courtesy of Holliday Farm.)

movement and knows where you are. If you cross-tie him, make sure the cross-ties are good and solid.

Whenever you lead him anywhere, use a halter shank; don't just take hold of his halter. And if you feel he's especially apt to spook or cut up, put the chain end of the shank through the near side-ring, up over his snout, and fasten it to the opposite side-ring. This will give you a little more "muscle" if he should try to rear or bolt. The average-sized person makes a poor anchor when a thousand-pound horse starts throwing his body around. A good sharp jerk on a chain over his nose, though, usually makes him see reason and respect authority again. No matter what all your friends do with *their* horses, then, remember that a lead shank, properly fastened, can mean the difference between a brief, mild blowup and a loose horse running in front of a truck.

Never ride along a high-speed, traffic-laden highway. If there's anything that makes me nervous, it's seeing someone riding casually along, two inches off the pavement, with a loose rein. If you *must* ride along a road, at least choose one that's lightly traveled and has good wide shoulders, and at least keep your horse in hand, so that if anything starts to happen you won't have to reel in three feet of rein before you can do anything about it.

Never tie your horse by the reins, and never tie him by anything to a piece of junk, a lawn chair, a porch railing, or anything the least bit breakable or movable. If you do, don't be surprised if all you find when you get back is some scattered bits and pieces and some tracks.

Don't take a horse out of his stall in the spring, or any time he's been cooped up and is busting his buttons, and just climb on. The laziest or best-mannered horse is going to feel higher than a kite on days like that, so don't expect him to be on his best behavior until he's had a little fling

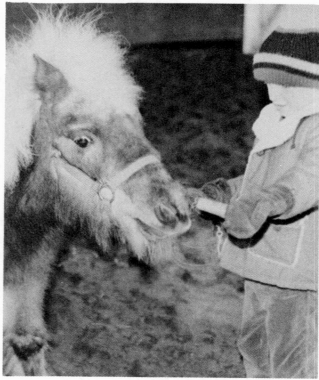

(ABOVE) A cold-backed horse or one that's simply been cooped up too long can be "ironed out" on the longe line before you ride. Wait until he's had his fill of bucking, kicking and playing and has settled down to a contented trot, like Scarlet Angel has. (RIGHT) We used up a whole bag of carrots to get this picture—just to show you what NOT to do! Jamie is enjoying treating Cocoa, and Cocoa is certainly enjoying being treated, but all in all it's safer not to encourage this sort of thing. (Photos by James Dandelski, courtesy of Holliday Farm.)

in the paddock or a session on the longe line first. There are even some horses that are always a little cold-backed and need some longeing first. If you see a space under the back of the saddle, then you'll know he "has a hump in his back" and is all set to play up. Get out the longe line.

Don't wrap it around your hand, though. I know several people who have done just that and wound up, when the fracas was over and the casualties counted, with a few more bruises and contusions to add to their collection. Water skiing behind a horse might be fun, but I suspect it's better with skis and water. Loop the line up, and then hold the entire thing in your hand, not just one side of the loop. This will enable you to let go, if prudence or necessity warrants it. Put the chain end of the longe line over the nose, as we described before and for the same reason. Also, it's always best to longe a horse in an enclosure, like the paddock or a pasture, just in case.

My advice about "looping" applies to lead shanks or ropes or anything else that could be extremely painful for you if a horse's sudden movement tightened it around your hand. Also watch out when you're tying your horse up; it can be just as painful to have your hand caught between a rope and a board. Ouch! Fortunately, a horse doesn't seem to realize that he has all that weight and strength at his command, but you'd better remember it.

Don't hand-feed your horse or let anyone else do it. This rule is hard to keep, because feeding a horse from your hand is so *nice*. But be warned! At first, a horse appreciates it; then he comes to expect it; third, he demands it. As pleasant as it is to feel his soft lips on your palm, this can lead to disaster in the form of ripped-off pockets and tooth-marked human flesh. And you can't blame the horse for it. He learns to expect what he's taught to expect.

Whether he's been hand-fed or not, never allow him to nibble on you or your clothing. Some people think this is charming—until the horse miscalculates and gets hold of some flesh. The first and any time he tries this with you, give him a quick pat on the muzzle and a sharp "No." The first time he tries you out with *any* "cute trick," in fact, reprimand him sharply. Some horses are never a bother, but a young or high-spirited, playful one probably will try something at least occasionally, just to see what happens.

Biting or trying to bite isn't necessarily a sign of orneriness. In a company of horses, nipping is often a way of playing or expressing affection, just as it is with pups and dogs. There is also what's known as reciprocal behavior among many animals, including horses. I know when I scratch my Chesapeake's back, he nibbles at my hand with his front teeth to show me he likes it and to "return the favor." Puppies, of course, chew on each other constantly. Horses will often stand in a pasture and scratch each other's backs or withers with their teeth, and of course they'll nip when they play together. This is so natural that even a well-trained horse might forget for a minute and bite at you playfully just to say "I love you" or "Thanks for scratching my neck." But no matter what his motive is, it can hurt. Discourage him. He might also kick up in your direction in a burst of playfulness someday. Let him know how you feel about that, too.

While we're on the subject of horses playing together, let me remind you not to let your horse crowd another one. All horses have definite personalities and very definite likes and dislikes. Never let your horse loose in a paddock or pasture with another horse, either, until you're very sure they're going to get along. One or the other of them will have to be dominant, and until that's settled, there may be some injurious "feeling out." This can take some time, especially for a horse used to being alone most of the time. Generally, I'm told, if two horses look each other over pretty carefully and then walk off and start grazing, they'll be all right. And when you see them scratching each other's withers, that usually means they're friends: one of them is dominant and the other has accepted the fact gracefully.

Here's a bit of advice that can save you a lot of sore toes. Make sure your horse is immediately and invariably responsive to "Whoa!" Professionally trained horses usually are, which is one reason I recommend them. Your horse should stop and stand at the word "whoa" under just about any circumstance short of World War III. He may tremble and snort and roll his eyes, but he should keep all four feet on the ground. If he won't, get someone to work on him, or do it yourself, until he will. It's essential, which is why well-trained horses learn this before and above all else. You'll come to know how your horse is feeling (they feel a lot more than they think); you'll learn when a softly murmured, soothing kind of "whoa" will work best, and when a good sharp one is required. And practice saying it, if you have to. Too many people have a very wishy-washy "whoa." *I* wouldn't pay any attention to it, either! So speak up when it's necessary. Be as sympathetic and as understanding as you can be, but sometimes when a horse is a little bit scared, it's a relief to him to hear the Voice of Authority—it means somebody is in charge.

There are lots of commonsense precautions you can take to avoid trouble. If you were able to find that "good barn" we've been talking about, you'll pick up a great many of them there, just by watching. Then put them into practice. Many a person has come to grief, or brought it to his horse, by being too casual or too ignorant or by showing off stupidly. I don't know anyone, however, who has ever gotten into trouble by being too careful. Don't take your little bumps and knuckle-skinnings too hard, but don't go out of your way looking for trouble, either.

Chapter Eleven: Nobody's Perfect

If you follow my advice and let an expert help you choose your first horse, he should have few if any minor faults, and no major ones. But since no horse is perfect, and since people have been known not to follow good advice, there's a possibility that your horse will have some built-in, ready-made problems for you to cope with.

There's the horse we've already mentioned, to get us started here, that persists in dancing about, backing up, or just plain walking off when you're trying to mount. If he won't park out for you, get a friend to help. We'll assume your horse isn't dangerous—that he means no harm and isn't going to kick at you. Get your friend to stand where the horse seems to want to go—behind if he's a backer, in front if he's a walker, and on the off side if he's a sidler. This should work if you're persistent. But make sure you're not causing the problem by pulling on the reins, giving him too much rein, poking him with your toe, kicking his rump as you swing across, or—heaven forbid—crashing down on him. Sometimes all it takes to cure a horse like this is to mount him properly often enough that he won't be expecting pain anymore.

Remember that any problem that has to do with training and manners may mean that the horse is still reacting to a bad experience with people. If it's only one small problem and the horse seems otherwise trusting and willing, the problem is well worth working on. But if his whole attitude is sour, he may simply not be safe for a beginner to handle because so many of his reactions are defensive ones. If you can see that even your love and kindness won't suffice to overcome his unhappy past, you'll be better off to admit it, sell him to someone more capable and experienced, and find a more agreeable horse for yourself. This will give both of you a better chance to make a go of it.

I can't say too often how important it is that your very first horse be particularly well trained, and that he stay that way for you. Some horses can be superbly mannered as long as they have a competent, authoritative rider aboard, but as soon as they discover this is not the case, they go hog wild with their newfound freedom. And it takes the average horse somewhere between two and five minutes to make this discovery. Ten minutes, and they've really got your number! This type of horse may take advantage of a beginner immediately, or he may bide his time and do it gradually, starting out well behaved and over the course of a few weeks turning from a Dr. Jekyll to a Mr. Hyde.

Here again, if you see this happening, admit it. It's no shame to make such a mistake. Not too many people new to the horse business choose an absolutely ideal horse the first time out. Even old-timers get surprised now and then. (There aren't that many ideal horses, anyway.) If you find that the horse you've bought is well trained but needs continual shaping up by your expert, you may decide to trade him for more of a beginner's horse. On the other hand, I know of instances in which girls have bought horses much too hot for them to manage, but they have simply hung in there, improved their riding with the help of a good teacher, and eventually caught up with their horses. You'll have to use your own judgment and that of your expert. Just don't feel terrible if you have to try another horse. It happens all the time.

Any horse that turns out to be a confirmed kicker or a serious biter or a crowder, or in any other way shows the results of bad experience to the point where he's dangerous, is also a prime candidate for a good old-fashioned horse trade. There is ample opportunity to get hurt by even a *friendly* horse, so for a beginner to try to cope with an unfriendly one is foolhardy. Don't waste time, money, feed and tears on a dangerous horse, either out of pride or in the hope that you can reform him. The risk isn't worth it, when there are so many wonderful horses that you can have fun with.

So much for some of the major problems. With any kind of luck, your horse will have only minor ones. There are some "stall vices," for instance, that you can learn to live with or deal with. Some horses "crib," which can be dangerous to them but not to you. They stand and chew on a stall-board edge or anything they can get a toothhold on (try to avoid such edges when you build), and a real cribber sucks in air while he does it. This is unattractive in the extreme—he often grunts, too—and, if he gets enough air in his stomach this way, he can become colicky, which is always hazardous. It doesn't help a horse that's already "a little heavey," either. You might be able to stop him, but in no time cribbing becomes a deeply ingrained habit.

It probably begins out of nervousness or sheer boredom, or it may be something as simple as new teeth coming in that starts it. The earlier you have a chance to catch it, the better. Paint any good chewing surface with creosote, if you can get it, or one of the sprays made for the purpose. There's even one made for dogs that might do it—it tastes perfectly awful. If that doesn't work, try a cribbing strap. You can get one through any of the major suppliers of tack and gear. The strap, properly adjusted, is fastened rather loosely around the horse's throttle. But when he cribs, or tries to, which requires him to tilt his head and flex hard at the throttle as he sucks in air, the strap becomes uncomfortably tight. If all else fails—or if you want to save time and effort by doing it first—remodel the stall so there's nothing for him to get hold of. He *has* to have something to grab with his teeth in order to crib.

Weaving is another fairly common stall vice. The horse just stands there and sways back and forth. If he only does it just before feeding time, I wouldn't worry about it. It's only harmful if he does it by the hour, persistently enough to lose flesh. You'd think, then, that a confirmed weaver would be thin when you first looked at him. Not necessarily. He may have been out in pasture, where horses seldom weave, and be hog-fat when you buy him. The only cure I know of for weaving is to let the horse out into his paddock or a pasture as often as you can.

About the same can be said for stall walking as for weaving, and some horses combine the two. Again, it can be just a preliminary to feeding time, and nothing to be overly concerned about, or it can be so persistent that you can't keep any fat on him—he "walks it off." And again, turning him out is the only thing I can suggest, but a walker might keep it up in the paddock, too. Once a horse has become a weaver or a stall walker, it's very hard to stop him. But you may be able to prevent his getting started by making sure he's well fed on a very regular schedule and doesn't have to worry about it. I suspect that most weavers and walkers did at one time have to worry about just that—when, or even if, their next meal was coming. Then see that he gets plenty of exercise and doesn't get bored to distraction.

Pawing is another stall vice that arises out of boredom more than anything else. This can be just as dangerous to your horse as cribbing, because he can lie down in the hollow he's dug in his stall and not be able to get his legs under him to get up again. Horses in this predicament are said to be "cast," and they often find this a terrifying experience. It's this fear that's so dangerous; as the horse thrashes about in his urgent efforts to rise, he can injure himself severely.

If your horse makes a habit of pawing large depressions into his stall floor or the sawdust, you should try to stop him. Get a couple of lightweight chains about eighteen inches long, and two wide, strong

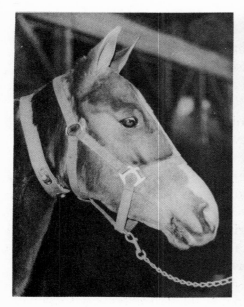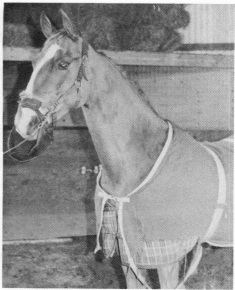

(LEFT) Chocolate doesn't need a cribbing strap, but we persuaded her to model one for us. This particular design has blunt metal studs that press into the neck only when the horse flexes strongly in order to crib. Otherwise, it's perfectly comfortable. (RIGHT) Squire Hall does need a blanket bib, as you can all too plainly see by the remnants of his top sheet. He can eat and drink just fine while wearing this contraption, by the way; he just can't tear up his expensive clothing. (Photos by James Dandelski, courtesy of Holliday Farm.)

leather dog collars with sturdy buckles. You'll also need two heavy double-ended trigger snaps. First, cut the collars down until they fit around your horse's pasterns, punching new holes to accommodate the shorter length. You should pad the collars with nylon "sheepskin," too, to make them comfortable. Put a collar on each of the horse's front pasterns. The collars should fit just snugly enough to keep them in place, but not tightly. Finally, snap a chain onto each collar buckle. Then, when the horse tries to paw, the chain will swing around and discourage him. (Not Mark, however—as you may have guessed. Mark unsnapped the chains somehow and hid them in the sawdust. He seemed to find it very entertaining to watch me hunt for them. One day when I simply could not find a missing chain, I gave Mark a long, strongly worded lecture before stomping off. The next morning I found the chain lying on the cement floor in front of his stall door. I have no idea how that happened, but it gives me an eerie feeling to this day!)

Horses that fling their heels too exuberantly in the stall can also injure themselves, either internally or by battering their legs. So if you find crescent-shaped dents high on the walls, you may want to put leg chains on his *hind* pasterns. This should at least lower his altitude somewhat.

Don't worry too much about the chains, or what people may say when they see them. They don't hurt the horse at all, and they might save him from serious injury. Watch him for a bit when you first put them on. He'll probably stand "rooted to the spot" for a while, as if he'd been nailed to the floor. But then he'll sniff and investigate and poke, and soon he'll be like Mark, who didn't even notice the chains. Of course as soon as good weather arrives, he can go outside, and the problem—boredom again—should solve itself.

If you put a sheet or a blanket on your horse, he may never bother it at all—or he may spend all his spare time "bothering" it. Here again, I really suspect that it's the high-spirited, playful, energetic horse, the kind that gets bored easily, that causes the most trouble. Little Mark went naked when he came to my barn, principally because I had run out of sheet money. No matter how snugly his sheet was buckled or how many ropes were tied under his tail, in ten minutes or less he was wearing it around his head in tattered strips, like a bunch of fringed neck scarves. I took the easiest way out by simply refusing to give him any more sheets to destroy. But if you have a special reason for having to keep your horse covered, and he acts like Mark did, there is a solution. It's called a blanket bib. It looks like a heavy, stiff leather scoop, with snaps that fasten it to the bottom of the halter. If you use one, be prepared for some strange comments from visitors, because everybody seems to have a different guess as to "what that thing is for," although the most frequent guess is that it's to keep the horse from biting you! But just ignore all that—sheets and blankets, as we mentioned before, are too expensive to use for fodder. And don't feel sorry for him—he brought it on himself, and anyway he'll soon be finding little games to play with it, like scooping up dirty sawdust—or worse yet, water—and spraying you with it.

Another problem that's minor in an otherwise well-mannered horse and most often crops up during bad weather is "cabin fever," or what we around here sometimes refer to as being stall crazy. A well-fenced, safe paddock attached to the barn will go a long way toward preventing stall-craziness. Just leave the door open every day that you can—every day that the wind-chill factor isn't fifty below, or something really nasty like that. I know horses that can "stand up" in the stall for weeks on end and come out safe enough to put a baby on right away. Mark, on the other hand, had to be "worked down" if he was forced to stay in his stall for two days in a row. Most are somewhere between these two.

One way to deal with this—and it's always a good idea when the horse has been shut in for a while—is to longe him or turn him loose to play for a few minutes before you saddle him up. We talked about this a little bit before. Most horses just want—and some need, desperately—a chance to kick up their heels, whinny, dash about, and generally "relieve their feelin's" before they're asked to be on their best behavior again. So let him. And don't be scared, watching him carry on like that. If he's well trained, as soon as he's gotten it all out of his system he'll be just as mannerly as he ever was, once the saddle's on. Just remember that every buck, rear and kick in the paddock or on the longe line is one fewer you have to worry about later. So be fair, if you have a spunky, well-trained horse like this, and don't ask him to be a perfect gentleman when he's positively bursting. Give him a chance—and save yourself a fall.

Another problem that isn't really a stall vice or exactly a training problem, either, but simply the result of one or two scares, is a horse's fear of narrow doorways. If yours pulls back and seems alarmed by a doorway, you can bet he's knocked his shoulder or hip on one, or caught a stirrup or harness strap, and was either hurt or badly frightened by the experience. Usually this can be corrected by great gobs of patience. Coax, plead, soothe, wheedle, and give him time to look the whole situation over and let himself be convinced that you're not as careless as someone else once was.

Refusing to enter a trailer, too, is usually the result of a scare, or perhaps just lack of experience. If you plan to show your horse at all, it'll be well worth your time to teach him to load and unload readily. And it *can* take time. If you own a trailer, just leave it in the paddock, ramp down, with a little grain on the ramp. He'll eat it. Then every day leave the grain farther inside. Eventually the trailer will be as familiar to him as his stall, and he won't be suspicious of it anymore. Otherwise, see if you can borrow a trailer for a day or two, and prepare to wait, coax, reassure and cajole. I know a couple of girls who spent three solid hours one day doing just that, but it really worked. A horse *can* be forced into a trailer, but that takes an expert with some pretty expert help. Although it may be necessary at times (when you don't have three hours to coax!), in the long run it may do more harm than good if it just confirms the horse's original opinion that trailers are scary things to be avoided at all costs.

Now, don't start thinking that all horses are vice-ridden creatures that spend most of their waking hours devising new ways to perplex you. Most horses have no real vices, and very few have more than one. You may have no problems like this to deal with at all. But you can see now that even if you do, it isn't necessarily the end of the world.

Nobody's perfect, so don't expect perfection. Be prepared to cope a little, just as you do with any good friend who irks you in some ways. But be reasonable about it. You may own several horses during your lifetime, each with its own character and personality. But your very first horse should be a wonderful adventure—an encouraging experience that will leave you with happy memories. So, if worse comes to worst and your expert decides that your horse is actually a danger to you, or more trouble than he's worth, buy another horse, and think of *him* as number one! Chances are you'll be very glad you did.

Chapter Twelve:
The Goofy Kid
and His Friends

Most really horse happy people would be very happy with most happy horses. But on occasion there's a personality clash. Horses definitely have personalities, just as people do, and some may suit you better than others. I've had quite a few discussions with my horse-minded friends about this, and one thing we all agree on is that these equine personalities can be very hard to describe and categorize. I'd like to try, anyway, and maybe you can be on the lookout for some of them as you go about your horse-hunting.

The best way I can think of is to hark back to some of the horses I have known. (You'll notice that I didn't say "known and loved." Some I have known and loved; some I have just known. I'm not a "horse lover," indiscriminately. In fact, I've been unable even to use that term since I read James Thurber's description of a dog lover as "a dog who is in love with another dog.")

However and regardless, here is just a sampling of some of the equine characters you may run across in your travels.

The Goofy Kid. This kind of horse is probably still quite young, though some—like Mark and Squire Hall, another Saddlebred gelding—retain their goofiness to the grave. Squire Hall, for instance, is six years old now, and typical of this category. He likes to pretend he's fierce, flattening his ears, snaking his neck and striking at his stall door when he gets a visitor, for all the world giving the impression that one would be well advised to enter his stall equipped with a large whip, a chair and a pistol.

Actually, however, he's a positive pussycat (he adores cats, by the way), once his bluff is called. Although he continues to play and pester all the time you're in his stall, pretending he's going to bite, and so on, he really wouldn't dream of harming a hair on your head. If you take his "menacing" for what it's worth, and smack him one in the snout when he gets carried away with his act, you'll be the best of friends. The right kind of person for this kind of clown has a good sense of humor, is calm

102

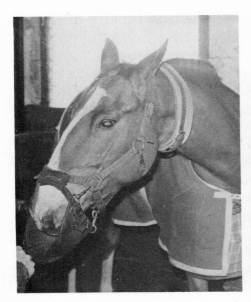 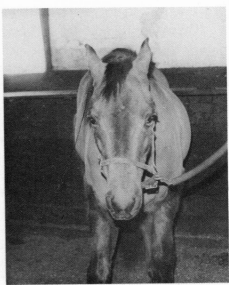

(LEFT) Squire Hall is perhaps the ultimate Goofy Kid. He goes into this little act—ears flat, threatening to bite—anytime anyone will pay attention—but it's really one hundred percent bluff. He's never harmed a soul. (RIGHT) Archie demonstrates the typical "Go away and leave me alone with my misery" expression of the Strong Silent Type—when he can be bothered to show any expression at all. (Photos by James Dandelski, courtesy of Holliday Farm.)

by nature, and is not easily buffaloed. Anybody else would be scared right out of the stall. In that case, Goofy's feelings would be hurt initially, and eventually, pleased as punch with the success of his play-acting, he'd be King Kong.

The Strong, Silent Type. He's just about the opposite of the Goofy Kid. Instead of menacing you, or doing much of anything else, he's more likely to stand in a corner, brooding, or just contemplating a knothole. His eyelids won't even flicker if you speak to him, although occasionally a faintly disgusted look may drift across his face. This kind of horse is baffling, because you never know what to expect from him, having no signs to read.

I remember one such horse that was like this twenty-four hours a day. The End of the World wouldn't have made much of an impression on him, and I never knew what he was thinking, although I often wondered. He certainly spent a lot of time mulling it over, whatever it was. Another one, a little spotted mare, was like this in the stall or cross-ties, but under saddle her head snapped up, her ears twirled, and she was all systems go. Maybe she really doesn't belong in this category;

as I say, it's hard to tell sometimes. But for the first type—the really consistent deadhead—I'd suggest an owner who doesn't like surprises. He's definitely not for a person looking to a horse for companionship, as most likely he won't even notice you're there. Goofy would make a better companion; even though he's a pest, at least there's no doubt that he's aware of your existence, and he really cares. You couldn't hurt Strong Silent's feelings with a crowbar.

The Love Bug. This one's passionately fond of people. Mia Mia, my example, was a 17-hand mare that not only loved people, she loved how they tasted. After five minutes in her stall, your hair was ruined and you needed a dry change of clothes. Being licked and kissed by a horse is certainly preferable to being bitten or stomped, of course, but it can get messy. Mia was also a little timid, and because she was so peopley, her reaction to one of her little frights was to try to climb into the lap of the nearest person, for "protection." This may be considered a handicap, a 17-hand horse not really fitting into anybody's lap. But she was so loving, it was impossible not to love her right back.

Almost anyone would be happy with a horse like Mia, except possibly overly fastidious types who are afraid of a few horse germs. But being a horse owner isn't for the extremely fastidious, anyway—as I remarked to a friend one day when I had my whole hand in a horse's mouth, feeling around for a wolf tooth.

Old Unreliable. Some of these are just great, like the little mare who was so quiet and safe to work around and then came to life under saddle. But most aren't that *dependably* unreliable. The worst ones are those whose personality depends on the mood of the moment, or how their breakfast is settling—and who, moreover, are sneaky about it, switching personalities with no warning at all. Sometimes you can recognize these by their shifty eyes, in which case you're lucky. Others have unbelievably angelic expressions. Judging by their enormous, limpid brown eyes (somewhat like a cocker spaniel's), they wouldn't *dream* of shying, bolting, or doing any of those bad things that some other horses do. And some days they wouldn't. Other days, they'll hit the ceiling if you sneeze. Now, this is the horse for people who *do* like surprises. Nobody was ever bored, for long, by an Old Unreliable.

The Pushbutton Horse. This is the one that's so well trained and so utterly dependable by nature that all riding instructors would give their only child for one—if they could *find* one. They're rare, but you'll see them in equitation classes for kids ten and under. Watching them, you get the feeling that if the rider fell off as he came in the gate, the horse would calmly finish all the figures perfectly. Edna Kay was a sterling example. I'd see her every year at the show, and every year her back was a little lower and her potbelly was a little pottier—and every two or three years she had a new infant aboard—but I never once saw her put a foot down wrong. Horses like her are literally priceless, because nobody who owns one would ever sell it.

These are a few, then. See how many more you can identify, and make up your own list.

And if you're beginning to think that horses are pretty strange animals—what on earth do you imagine they must think of *people?*

No matter which personality type your own very first horse is, *care* is the key word in your relationship with him. Take care in choosing him; then take good care of him. You have to care a lot. There's hard work to owning a horse. I myself have put in my time operating a manure fork, and my friends at the stable work like—well, like horses. But we don't mind, because we find it enormously rewarding. We care. We *love* horses. We are, in plain fact, horse happy.

May you be the same, always.

Glossary

- **ACTION.** A horse's way of using its legs is called its *action* or *motion*. A gait requiring a great deal of action is called an animated gait.
- **AGED.** A horse over nine years old.
- **ANGLO-ARAB.** A horse that is half Thoroughbred and half Arabian. There is a registry for Anglo-Arabs.
- **APPALOOSA.** A breed of horses, many of which have very distinctive markings, found among the Nez Perce Indians of North America by early white explorers. Ancient oriental artwork also depicts horses marked this way. The "Appie" is hardy and good-tempered.
- **ARABIAN.** An ancient breed originating in the arid lands around the Mediterranean. Arabians are noted for their delicate beauty and their stamina and spirit. Most of the well-known light horse breeds today can trace part of their ancestry to the Arabian or one of its similar early variations, such as the Barb and the Turk.
- **BALD FACED.** A horse with a wide white strip, or *blaze*, down its face. The blaze widens to include the nostrils and sometimes the whole muzzle and/or the eyes.
- **BARREL.** A horse's body from hips to shoulders. In the old days this was sometimes called the "middle piece."
- **BARREN.** A barren mare is one that is not pregnant. Sometimes the word is used to describe a mare that is just not in foal at the moment; and sometimes it is used to describe a mare that for some reason is not able to carry a foal at all. In the first case, it would probably be said that the mare is "barren this season" or "open this season."
- **BAY.** A bay horse is reddish brown with black legs, mane and tail. There are various shades of bay, including blood bay, bright bay, rusty bay and mahogany bay.
- **BILLET.** On a hunt or saddle seat saddle, the sturdy straps, sewn in under the edge of the seat, to which the girth is attached. These should be checked frequently for signs of wear and weakness. Most saddles have three billets on each side; some have four.
- **BLACK.** A horse is considered black only when no brown hairs can be found on it at all. Such horses are rare.
- **BLANKET.** (1) A fairly heavy covering made to fit a horse's body from tail to chest. Weights, materials and designs vary a great deal. Most blankets buckle at the chest and have two belly straps. When buying a blanket, measure your horse from withers to tail,

and then *specify* that this is the measurement you are giving. A horse with a 54-inch back, for example, would require a 72-inch blanket, since the blanket size includes the part that covers the chest. (2) "Blanket" is also used to describe the large white area on the rump and back of an otherwise dark colored Appaloosa.
- **BLAZE.** The relatively wide white strip down a horse's face. (A narrower white strip is called a *stripe*.)
- **BOLT.** A horse bolts when it runs off with its rider. A horse may bolt from fright once or twice in its life; or bolting may be a trick it has picked up to get its own way. If the latter is true, some stern retraining by an experienced horseman is indicated.
- **BRAN.** The husks of wheat grains, fed to horses as a laxative and a coat conditioner. Horses allowed to graze on good pasture probably won't need a laxative, but if their diet is solely hay and grain, they might, especially if they don't get much exercise.
- **BREED TRAITS.** Characteristics generally considered to be typical of a given breed. Docility might be a breed trait, for instance; or a short back, or a tendency to pace rather than trot.
- **BUCK.** When a horse bucks, it puts its head down, arches its back upward, and hops into the air—usually several times in succession. The careful trainer knows that bucking is essentially a fear reaction and tries never to frighten a young horse. A horse that has never been frightened by a rider rarely learns to buck.
- **BUCKSKIN.** A golden coat color—ranging from a pale, creamy shade to a deep "antique gold"—accompanied by black legs, mane, tail and dorsal stripe.
- **CALKS.** Small bits of metal attached to the heel and/or toe of a horseshoe to increase traction in mud or snow and ice. The old-timers referred to these as "corks."
- **CANTER.** A collected three-beat gait, ranging from the lightly controlled canter of the English pleasure horse to the spectacular high-rolling canter of the Tennessee Walker.
- **CANTLE.** On an English saddle, the slightly raised rear portion of the seat. On a stock saddle, the cantle is raised somewhat higher and is often flared out as well.
- **CAST.** When a horse is down and can't get up again without aid, it is said to be *cast*. When this happens, the horse must be helped up by its caretakers, by means of ropes, leverage boards, and whatever else

is required. It is very important to keep the horse calm during this procedure, or it might panic and injure itself or those who are trying to help.

- CAVESSON. When used with a full bridle, the cavesson is a noseband fitting snugly about two-thirds of the way down a horse's face, with a thin headstall that runs around the ears through the loop in the browband. The cavesson helps keep a horse from "yawning" and trying to evade the action of the bits.
- CHESTNUT. A chestnut horse has a reddish brown coat, with mane, tail and legs of the same or a lighter color. As with bays, chestnut shades vary greatly—from light, golden tones through reds to dark reddish-brown shades. Very dark chestnuts may be called liver chestnuts. Westerners call red chestnuts *sorrels*.
- CINCH. The girth on a stock saddle, from the Spanish *cincha*.
- COARSE (as opposed to *fine*). A horse with thick bones and a generally heavy, unrefined appearance is said to be *coarse*. Sometimes only the head is at fault, in which case it is "coarse-headed."
- Coarseness is a matter of opinion, and it is judged according to breed and intended use. A heavy hunter, for example, is required to have big bones, and, rather than being coarse, it "has a lot of substance."
- COLIC. A general term referring to any acute pain in the abdominal region. This pain can be caused by a buildup of gas (horses are unable to burp), an obstruction somewhere along the line, or a "twisted gut" (see entry for TWISTED GUT). Since colic is very painful and can be fatal, the horse owner must always be alert for signs of discomfort and be prepared to call the vet at once.
- COLLECTION. "Gathering a horse together" by using the bit or bits and leg control and by shifting your body weight. The greater the collection, the more precisely the horse will perform.
- COLT. A male horse from birth to about four years old.
- CONFORMATION. A horse's conformation is simply its shape or figure. Different breeds have slightly different ideals in conformation—otherwise we couldn't tell one breed from another—but some attributes, like balance and proportion, are universally desired. Since there is no absolutely ideal horse, conformation judging is largely a matter of comparing faults.
- COOLER. A large covering that is put over a hot horse to keep it from cooling out too rapidly. (I've always thought these should be called "warmers"!) A cooler should be of a weight suitable for the air temperature at the time and should wrap around the horse's neck and chest, covering it completely from tail to ears.
- CORONET. The line at the top of a horse's hoof where hoof wall and leg hair meet. This is where the hoof wall grows (from the top), so if you use hoof dressing, it will do the most good here.
- COW-HOCKED. A conformation fault, considered a weakness, in which a horse's hocks point toward each other slightly, like a cow's. This in turn causes the hind feet to point slightly away from each other, or to toe out. A cow-hocked horse would not have a very pretty stance or gait and would probably not be quite as strong as a straight-legged horse.
- CRIBBING. A stall vice in which the horse grabs hold of the edge of something, flexes its neck hard, and sucks in air. This is dangerous as well as unsightly, since the horse may give itself colic. It is also hard on the stall boards, so a cribbing strap should be tried, if you can't rebuild the stall to eliminate inside edges suitable for grabbing.
- CROSS-TIES. Two sturdy chains with snaps at one end for the halter side-rings, and at the other end for heavy ring-bolts firmly fastened into the walls. When a horse is cross-tied, he's ready for grooming, shoeing, vetting or what-have-you. Every stable needs at least one set of cross-ties.
- CROUP. A horse's back from the point of the hips to the tail. This is a rather important conformation point, as a croup that drops off sharply ("goose-rumped") is unattractive and may adversely affect the horse's gait and balance.
- CROWDING (in the stall). The horse "crowds" his caretaker, in the stall or in cross-ties, by pushing over against him. This is a bad habit, whether the horse means ill or not, as there's always the possibility of your being stepped on, if not kicked. Find something with a mildly pointed end, hold it steady, and let him crowd into *that* once or twice.
- CURB BIT. A bit with a long shank or *cheek* that works with a chain or strap on the leverage principle. It applies pressure to the bars of the jaw as well as to the mouth itself. It may be used alone, with a stock seat outfit, or in conjunction with a snaffle, in a full bridle.
- DAM. A horse's mother.
- DOCK. The point at which the tail meets the croup. Also, the upper end of the tail itself.
- DOUBLE BRIDLE. (See FULL BRIDLE.)
- EQUITATION. The art of riding a horse.
- FARRIER. A person who shoes horses.
- FENDER. The part of a stock saddle to which the stirrup is attached and which also protects the rider's legs.
- FETLOCK. The "ankle" joint, between the pastern and the cannon bone. Often the longer hair that grows here is also referred to as the fetlock.
- FIGURES. The patterns that equitation riders are required to follow, such as a serpentine or a figure eight.
- FILLY. A female horse from birth to about four years old.
- FINE (as opposed to *coarse*). A fine horse has delicate legs, head, neck, etc. Again, the desirability of fineness or coarseness depends on breed and intended use. A Saddle Horse is expected to be finer than a Walker, for instance.
- FINE HARNESS HORSE. A Saddle Horse, shown to a show cart in fine (delicately made) harness. It is required to do an animated walk and an animated park trot. Shown with full mane and tail.
- FIVE-GAITED HORSE. An American Saddle Horse that

has been trained to execute the animated walk, trot, canter, slow-gait and rack. Shown with full mane and tail.

- **FLANK.** The area between the point of the hip and the rib cage. This area is very tender and should be groomed gently.
- **FULL BRIDLE.** A bridle designed for use with two bits, a curb and a light snaffle.
- **GIRTH.** (1) Of a saddle: the leather, web or string strap that holds the saddle on the horse. (2) Of a horse: the circumference of the barrel, just behind the elbows.
- **GRAY.** A coat color in which white hairs are interspersed with black hairs to produce an overall gray appearance (steel gray) or an overall white appearance with darker areas such as dapples, dark legs, or just dark hocks and knees.
- **HACKAMORE.** A type of bridle, either bitless or used with a bit that controls by pressing directly under the jaw instead of in the mouth. Entirely bitless hackamores control a horse by means of a heavy noseband that presses on the bridge of its nose.
- **HALTER.** A leather, nylon or rope headstall used for leading or tying a horse.
- **HAND.** A unit for measuring how high a horse stands (the distance from the ground to the top of the withers). One hand equals four inches.
- **HAND GALLOP.** A moderately slow gallop, or fast canter, in which the horse is somewhat collected ("in hand").
- **HAY BELLY.** The large "potbelly" that some horses acquire when fed too much hay and too little grain.
- **HEAD-SET** (or **HEADSET**). How the horse holds its head and neck; its *carriage.*
- **HEADSTALL.** The principal parts of a bridle, usually consisting of cheek pieces, crown piece, browband and throatlatch.
- **HEAVES.** Emphysema, a chronic lung disorder that is indicated by a dry, sharp cough and a heaving of the flanks. It is sometimes called broken wind, because when a heavey horse exhales, often the air is expelled in two stages, with a very brief break in between. This can be seen by watching the flanks move. If you suspect a horse you're considering buying of being "a little heavey," ask to have him worked at speed for a while, and then watch him breathe.
- **HOCK.** The large, important joint in the hind leg, at the "crook." The horse's gait depends a great deal on the conformation and strength of the hock.
- **HOOF DRESSING.** A thick, oily paste to be applied to dry hooves, especially around the coronet bands. Healthy hooves should need very little or no dressing. This term might also be used for a material applied just before a show to polish the hooves.
- **HOOF PICK.** A small tool used to clean out a horse's hooves, with a blunt point for the crevices. Many people find it handier to use a bent screwdriver.
- **HORN.** On a stock saddle, the horn is the small knob on top of the pommel. It's good for tying a rope to, or for an emergency "handle" when legs and balance fail!

- **HUNTER.** A general term for a type of horse that is trained for cross-country riding and moderate jumping. Hunters can range in size from ponies to very large, heavy horses. Most full-sized hunters have at least some Thoroughbred blood, and many are registered Thoroughbreds. Since hunters are expected to jump—although usually not as strenuously as stadium jumpers—they should have quite big bones. High withers help, too.
- **JOG.** The jog trot, a slow, easy trot with little or no action, used mostly with western-type horses.
- **JUMPER.** A horse used for jumping obstacles. Unlike the hunter, the jumper is not necessarily required to have good manners, or even to have good conformation, although many do. Jumper classes generally feature higher and more difficult obstacles than hunter classes, and they may also be timed, especially in "jump-offs," when two or more jumpers are tied. Jumpers may be of any breed or combination of breeds, as long as they are willing and able.
- **LAMINITIS** (also called *founder*). This is a very serious, painful, and often crippling inflammation of a horse's hoof. In most cases, both front hooves are affected. The cause is not always certain, but founder seems most often to be the result of getting into the grain bin; or being overheated and then allowed to cool out too rapidly, to eat and/or to drink water too soon. It might also follow a bout with a serious infection of some sort, or a case of colic. If your horse shows signs of pain in its forehooves (such as shifting them back and forth), put your bare hand on the wall of the hoof. If you feel heat, call your vet *immediately.* Nowadays there are means of combating laminitis if it is caught at the first signs, although a horse that has foundered is rarely as useful as before. If you see a horse whose hooves have ridges on them, it may have had laminitis at some time. You probably should not buy a horse that has had laminitis if you want one for hard or fast work.
- **LEAD.** When loping, cantering or galloping, a horse always leads with one side or the other—or, in the case of cross-cantering, with both sides. The leading legs, both front and rear, reach out first and farther than the opposing legs. Most horses favor one lead over the other and, if left to their own preference on a straightaway, will tend to use only that lead. When moving on an arc or in a circle, however, they will tend to use the lead toward the center, as this gives them the best balance and support.
- **LEAD SHANK** (also called a *halter shank*). A strip of strong leather six or seven feet long, with a chain (preferably brass) about a foot and a half long sewn to one end. On the end of the chain is a very strong trigger snap for attaching to the halter. No horse barn should be without at least one lead shank.
- **LIGHT HORSE BREEDS.** Breeds used for riding, as opposed to *heavy horse breeds*, or draft horses.
- **LIVER CHESTNUT.** A dark brown coat color, sometimes with red and gold highlights. A liver chestnut horse has a mane and tail no darker than the body color.
- **LONGE.** To put a long line (longe line) on a horse's

halter and move him about you in a circle, usually at a trot. Longeing is good for exercising a horse when you don't feel like riding it; for getting the rough edges off a frisky one *before* you ride it; for strengthening a horse's legs and wind; and for exercising and schooling young horses still unable to carry weight on their backs every day. You'll often hear people say *lunge* instead of *longe*, and this is now generally accepted as meaning the same thing. (I even saw a classified ad in our newspaper recently offering a young horse for sale that was "trained to lead and *lounge*." But either that was a misprint, or the owner was being unusually honest!)

- LOPE. A natural gait for most horses, the lope is most easily defined by comparing it to other gaits: it is the same as a gallop, but slower; the same as a canter, but less collected. A nice, easy, rather slow, three-beat gait.

- MARE. An adult female horse at least four years old.

- MORGAN. A breed of horse developed in New England for general riding, driving and farmwork. Quite a bit larger than its pony-sized forebears, in many ways it still resembles the fabled Justin Morgan, a stallion reputed to be the principal founding sire of the breed. The breed nearly became extinct in the nineteenth century, but governmental intervention and the infusion of Saddlebred blood brought it back. This has created two factions among Morgan fanciers: those who decry the infusion and prefer the "old-timey" Morgans; and those who favor the somewhat larger, flashier Saddlebred crosses that are so popular in today's Park Morgan classes.

- MUZZLE. A horse's muzzle is the area that includes the mouth, chin and nostrils. The size of the muzzle—the smaller the better—used to be one of the criteria for judging a "blood horse." To say that a horse could "drink out of a tin cup" was high praise. By contrast, it was said of Hambletonian, a coarse-appearing animal, that he "couldn't have drunk out of anything smaller than a half-bushel measure!"

- NAVICULAR DISEASE. A tragic hoof ailment in which the hoof simply deteriorates. Eventually the horse must be put to sleep. It seems to result from the bruising of the sole and of the tiny navicular bone in the center of the hoof just above the sole. This can be caused by stepping hard on a stone, or perhaps even by habitually being worked on a hard surface. If you must ride your horse on stony ground or on hard surfaces, leather pads may prevent bruises. (See PADS.)

- OVER AT THE KNEE. This is a conformation fault in which, when viewed from the side, a horse's knee joint can be seen to jut forward slightly. Usually both forelegs are affected. It may be a natural defect, or it may be the result of overwork at an early age (as in some racehorses). It should be considered a fairly serious fault, since it is a weakness.

- PACE. Used generally, *pace* may mean any gait, as in "putting a horse through its paces." Usually, however, the word is used to describe a particular gait, the *pace*, in which the two legs on the same side move forward and back in unison (that is why it's referred to as a "lateral" gait). The only breed (in America) in which this gait is encouraged is the Standardbred, our harness-racing horse. Today pacers far outnumber trotters in that breed.

- PADDLE. This is a faulty gait in which the horse's hind feet "paddle" outward as he trots. This is sometimes caused by faulty conformation and sometimes simply by bad shoeing. If the problem isn't very pronounced, it can often be corrected by having the hooves trimmed and shod to compensate.

- PADDOCK. The name given to a fenced enclosure too small to be called a pasture. Western folk might call the same area a corral.

- PADS. A pad of thick leather is sometimes cut into the exact shape of the bottom of the horse's hoof and inserted between the hoof and the shoe. Often this is done only on the front hooves, which bear much of the horse's weight. When pads are used, a resilient material like oakum and pine tar must also be inserted between the pad and the frog, to serve as a "shock absorber." Pads should be removed at regular intervals, and the hooves inspected, since disease or an abnormal condition can be hidden by the pads. Pads are most often used as protection against stone bruising, but can also be used to build up a hoof to a desired length, as in some show horses that need a longer hoof to achieve the required action. Pads can also be useful in the winter in preventing snow from packing up in the horse's cup-shaped hooves.

- PALOMINO. A palomino is a horse of a golden color—ideally "the color of a new penny"—with a white mane and tail. There are at least two registries in this country for palominos. Since the requirements for registration are much like those of some of the more established breeds in their earlier days, the palomino might be considered a "breed in the making" at this point. However, many horses registered as palominos are also listed in another breed registry, such as those for the quarter horse or the American Saddle Horse. These palominos are "double registered."

- PARK HORSE. "Park horse classes" in horse shows are, simply speaking, for horses whose degree of action and animation falls somewhere between that of the three- and five-gaited Saddlebreds and that of pleasure horses. Once in a great while a show will include park classes for Saddlebreds, but usually they are for Morgans and Arabians. "Park Morgans" and "Park Arabians" are expected to be flashier and more animated than their pleasure horse counterparts. Park horses are traditionally shown under saddle seat tack.

- PARK OUT. When shown at halter, or at the end of a performance class when the horses are lined up for the judges' final inspection, Morgans, Saddlebreds, Walkers and Hackneys are expected to *park out*—to stand perfectly still, with their hind legs extended behind the vertical. This serves the double purpose of showing off the horse's conformation to its best advantage, and tending to help keep the horse from moving. At home, the latter benefit also applies!

- **PAWING.** Most horses will occasionally paw at the ground, but one that makes a habit of it to the point where he gouges hollows in his stall floor must be discouraged lest he become cast. Horses that paw fretfully while you're trying to groom or mount them are a hazard too, because they might well strike you. In the first case, try letting the horse out or exercising it more; if that fails, try leg chains. In the second case, just say "No" or "Quit" sharply, and smack him every time he paws.

- **PELHAM BIT.** One of several varieties of bits, all of which consist basically of a single bar in the mouth, to which a curb chain or strap and a double set of reins can be attached.

- **PELHAM BRIDLE.** A bridle designed for use with a Pelham bit. It is usually a simple headstall with its own noseband or with a separate cavesson.

- **PINTO.** A spotted horse whose coat combines areas of white with areas of any other solid color.

- **PLATE.** A light, simple horseshoe, the kind most often used on pleasure horses.

- **PLEASURE DRIVING HORSE.** A horse trained to harness, but not for the extreme animation required of a fine harness horse. These horses have an easy, steady trot and are responsive to commands, standing quietly and backing readily.

- **PLEASURE HORSE.** Whether western pleasure, English pleasure, or a pleasure horse categorized by breed (such as pleasure Morgan), this horse should be a pleasure to ride—that is, willing, easy to control, and smooth-gaited. In recent years the Saddlebred pleasure horse classes at horse shows have become more and more like the three-gaited classes, resulting in the promotion and instant popularity of yet another class for Saddlebreds, the "country pleasure" class. Among Walking Horses, the counterpart of the easier-going country pleasure horse is called a "plantation Walker."

- **PONY OF THE AMERICAS (P.O.A.).** A breed of very sturdy, pony-sized horses. The P.O.A. is marked like its larger cousin, the Appaloosa, with the same wide variety of markings. P.O.A.s are entirely capable of carrying an adult rider, but since they were bred especially for youngsters and possess a temperament ideal for this purpose, adults are not allowed to ride them in P.O.A. shows.

- **POST.** When a rider "rises to the trot" by sitting down on the saddle only at every other beat, he is posting. A trot fast enough to require posting is called a *posting trot*. Posting makes things easier for both horse and rider, and it looks a whole lot better than bouncing!

- **PUREBRED.** A purebred horse is one whose ancestors, as far back as can be ascertained, are all of one breed.

- **QUARTER HORSE.** A breed first established in colonial times for sprinting. Back when clearing land for racetracks was all hard hand labor, the easiest way to do it was to clear a straight, narrow path through the woods—and a quarter mile was deemed long enough! The horses that raced on these tracks were called quarter pathers. Eventually they moved along westward with the pioneers and became renowned for their intelligence and agility in working cattle.

- **RACK.** One of the gaits of the five-gaited Saddle Horse, in which each of the four hooves strikes the ground at a different time, resulting in what is called a four-beat gait—and an extremely smooth ride.

- **REAR.** Rearing—rising high on its hind legs—is to be considered a vice, and a very hazardous one to both horse and rider. If your horse rears while you're on its back, throw your weight as far forward as you can and grab its neck. If it rears on a regular basis, either give it to a trainer to be "cured," or sell it.

- **REGISTERED.** Nowadays, with so many different kinds of registries, it's hard to say just what this term means. If your horse is registered with an established *breed* registry, then it's a purebred, and you can prove it. But it might be a "registered half-Arab," or a "registered pinto," or something else, and not be purebred at all. So when you're horse hunting and are told that a horse is "registered," find out: a registered *what?* And never pay good money for a so-called registered horse until you have the signed-over certificate in your hand.

- **RUNNING WALK.** This gait is peculiar to the Tennessee Walking Horse. It consists of a very fast "walk," with the head nodding noticeably (thus the term "Tennessee Nodder") and the action of the forelegs high and far-reaching, with the hind legs drawn well under in almost a squat. It all sounds awkward, but when done well, it is extremely smooth and flowing, with the horse's back hardly moving at all. There can be a definite difference in degree of animation between the "show Walker's" gait and that of the "plantation" or pleasure horse. The slower, more relaxed version of the gait should come naturally, with extensive training (and often some rather bizarre shoeing) required only for the show ring's demands.

- **SADDLEBRED.** A breed known officially as the American Saddle Horse. Developed by early Bluegrass horsemen, the Saddlebred is noted for great style and beauty, a keen, lively disposition, and an inherent tendency toward the four-beat gait.

- **SEAL BROWN.** A very dark brown coat color, sometimes actually black with only some brown edges.

- **SEASON (or HEAT).** A mare is said to be in season, or in heat, when she is at that point in her reproductive cycle during which, if bred, she can conceive a foal. This varies somewhat among individuals, but on the average a mare comes in season about every three weeks and remains in season for two or three days. During the winter months most mares don't come in season at all. Since the gestation period for horses is eleven months, this is Nature's way of attempting to prevent foals from being born in bitter-cold weather when grazing is poor or nonexistent.

- **SEAT.** This can be part of a term describing a riding style, as in "hunt seat," or it can refer to a rider's manner of sitting a horse. If someone says you have a good seat, he means that you look nice and seem secure.

• SHEET. A lightweight covering for a horse, designed the same as a blanket but not as warm. It can be used to keep a horse's coat short and smooth, and to protect a horse from flies in the summer.

• SHETLAND. A breed of small ponies that originated on the Shetland Islands. Of an ideal size for very young riders, they are nonetheless easily capable of carrying adults, as they are extremely strong and hardy. Because of the shaggy coats they grow, they are able to withstand nearly any kind of weather with only minimal shelter.

• SHOULDER. The plainly visible long, flat bone running from the upper side of the chest to the withers. You will see and hear frequent references to the much desired "sloping" or "well laid back" shoulder, but the only way to be able to recognize one when you see it is to compare a lot of shoulders. A "straight" or "upright" shoulder is frowned on because it restricts freedom of movement. A horse with such shoulders has a rougher gait, and so is also more susceptible to lameness than one with a good shoulder.

• SHY. (This is a verb, not an adjective.) A horse *shies* when it changes direction abruptly because it sees or hears something that alarms it. Shying may be followed by bolting, but not if you're careful to maintain contact with the horse's mouth so you can react swiftly, no matter how surprised *you* are. Most horses will shy at something, sometime, but one that's startled by everything under the sun is usually more trouble than it's worth and might best be traded for one that's less excitable.

• SINGLEFOOT. Any natural, four-beat gait. A Saddle Horse breeder, seeing this in a colt, would probably call it *ambling* and would develop it into a slow-gait and rack, while the western-type horse owner would probably be content to call it a singlefoot and enjoy it.

• SIRE. A horse's father. When used as a verb, "to sire" means to father.

• SLOW-GAIT. Another four-beat gait, about which there is some controversy and not a little confusion. Originally, a show horse could execute as its slow-gait any one of several four-beat gaits, such as the amble or the stepping pace. This is still the case, but many people claim that most gaited horses nowadays simply perform a slower, more controlled version of the rack when asked to slow-gait. (It takes an experienced eye to tell any of these gaits apart.)

• SNAFFLE BIT. Probably the simplest of all bits, the snaffle is just a solid or jointed bar with a ring on each end for the reins. While there are many versions of the snaffle bit (such as twisted wire, copper wound, etc.), they all work the same way—by exerting pressure on only the corners of the mouth.

• SNAFFLE BRIDLE. A bridle designed for use with a snaffle bit. It consists of a simple headstall, either with its own noseband or with a separate cavesson.

• SOCK. Most people consider a horse to have a "sock"

when its leg is white from the hoof to anywhere up to about halfway to the knee or hock.

• SOLE. The major part of the bottom surface of a horse's hoof, surrounding the frog. Never scrape the sole too hard when you're cleaning hooves. Any trimming of the sole should be left to a farrier or vet.

• SORREL. When someone accustomed to speaking of stock horses says sorrel, he means a chestnut (see CHESTNUT). The terms are interchangeable.

• SOUND. A sound horse is free of lameness, disease, or afflictions of any kind.

• SOUR, or SOUR-EARED. A horse with a surly or suspicious outlook on life often has its ears laid back and is sometimes said to be "sour-eared." It is wise to keep an eye on such a horse because it's a sign that he is apprehensive or grumpy about something. Most horses do this now and then, when an appropriate occasion arises, but one with habitually sour ears is one you'd do well to leave alone.

• SPOOK. This means the same thing as *shy*, and a spooky horse is one that shies on a regular basis. A spooky horse and a beginning rider are not the best combination in the world, since many beginning riders are a bit spooky, too. A spooky horse needs a calm, reassuring rider, and vice versa.

• STALLION. Any adult, uncastrated (or "entire") male horse.

• STANDARDBRED. A breed of horse developed in America. Originally it was called the American Trotting Bred Horse, as the purpose then was to develop a fast trotter. The earlier specimens that paced naturally were discouraged from doing so if at all possible, as it had been decreed that "no gentleman drives a pacer." So much pacing blood went into the breed, however, that it was a constant battle to eliminate this tendency. Later on, at the harness tracks, pacers were in disfavor among bettors because of their predilection for breaking gait—and losing races—when pressed hard for speed. But the invention and acceptance of the pacing hobble, which works very effectively to keep the pacer on gait, changed all that. Now the great majority of harness races in this country are for pacers.

• STAR. A small white spot of any shape on a horse's forehead.

• STIRRUP IRON and STIRRUP LEATHER. On a hunt or saddle seat saddle, the stirrup consists of two parts: the leather strap, called the stirrup leather; and the metal part, called the stirrup iron (although most are stainless steel these days).

• STOCKING. A white leg marking in which the white extends from the hoof to more than halfway to the knee or hock.

• STRIDE. A horse may be long-strided or short-strided, depending on the amount of ground covered at each step in relation to its size.

• STRIKE. Striking is a vice in which a horse "strikes out" with a forehoof. If he just stands in his stall and strikes the door for food or attention, it's a rather minor vice (if the door is sturdy!); but if he strikes at people, "with malicious intent," it's a major one.

- STRIPE. A face marking, narrower than a blaze.
- STUD. A stallion used for breeding.
- SWAYBACKED. If a horse's spine sags in the middle, the horse is swaybacked. This may be forgiven in an old horse, but in a young or middle-aged one, the shorter and straighter the spine, the better and stronger.
- SWEAT SCRAPER. A handy tool, the sweat scraper can be used to—well, scrape sweat; or it can be used to scrape off excess water when bathing your horse. It's even handier if it has a shedding blade on one side—tiny teeth that will remove dead hair at shedding times.
- TENNESSEE WALKING HORSE. A breed developed primarily in or near Tennessee, at approximately the same time the Saddle Horse was being developed in and around Kentucky. In fact, the two breeds shared many of their earliest ancestors; but while the Kentuckians developed the pacing tendency into the slow-gait and rack, and refined their "Saddlers," the Tennesseans perfected the famous running walk and developed a coarser, extremely docile and tolerant horse, eminently suitable for comfortable, all-day tours of the plantations.
- THOROUGHBRED. The only correct usage of this word in regard to horses is in reference to the specific breed developed first in England with one purpose in mind—to run faster than any other horse in the world, at a distance. This it did, and still does. Today, the Thoroughbred is also popular as a hunter, and crosses between Thoroughbreds and draft or coach horses are very popular too, as "heavy" hunters.
- THREE-GAITED HORSE. Sometimes called a "walk-trot" horse, the three-gaited horse is an American Saddle Horse that is trained to show at three gaits: the animated walk, the trot and the canter. In a general way, walk-trots tend to be finer and to go higher and slower than gaited horses. They are shown with mane removed and tail thinned, to accentuate fineness. (To ask the owner of a Saddlebred, "Are you going to trim him?" is to ask if he plans to show the horse three-gaited, since all other Saddlebred performance classes require a full mane and tail. Most saddle seat equitation Saddlebreds are also "trimmed" these days.)
- THRUSH. Thrush is a particularly nasty, evil-smelling disease of the hoof, affecting both the sole and the frog. What it amounts to is that the foot is decaying, and that's what it smells like. If noticed at the onset of the problem, it may be cured easily, or it may persist; if not noticed soon, it will surely persist, and at worst can even mean the destruction of the horse. Since rotting is involved, obviously there is too much moisture somewhere. Either the horse has been standing in mud or in a low, wet pasture too much, or his stall has been wet and dirty too long. Avoid these situations and you'll probably avoid thrush too, unless you bought it with the horse. In any event, get a vet's help at once, and be very conscientious about following his instructions.

- TROT. The two-beat diagonal gait natural to most horses, in which the two legs on opposite corners move in unison.
- TWISTED GUT. This is a very severe problem in which a horse's intestine becomes twisted, causing extreme pain. Often this happens when a horse thrashes about unattended in the throes of colic (you should keep him on his feet and moving to avoid this); or in the throes of panic when he's cast himself. Of course, only a vet can diagnose twisted gut. While modern surgical procedures have saved many horses that would have died only a few years ago, the prognosis is still usually bleak. It's very important, therefore, to feed, water and cool your horse very carefully, and not to let him paw holes in his stall where he can cast himself.
- VICE. A term applied to any unpleasant or dangerous habit a horse may have.
- WEANLING. A colt or filly is called a weanling from the time it is weaned from its mother (generally at about six months) until it is a year old.
- WEAVING. A stall vice in which the horse sways its head and neck from side to side without moving its feet. Some horses weave slightly and infrequently. Some, however, weave so hard as to almost rock themselves off their feet, and do it by the hour, in which case it becomes a troublesome vice. (I know a mare that weaves, to all appearances, in perfect time to whatever tune the barn radio plays!) A confirmed weaver is virtually incurable, but turning it out into a paddock or pasture might help—until you put it back into the stall again.
- WHISKERS. When we say a horse's whiskers must be trimmed for showing, we mean its chin whiskers (which can become amazingly long) and also its eyebrows—those long, fine hairs growing just above and below the eyes (*not* the eyelashes!). Extreme care must be taken when using clippers or scissors on the eyebrows, as any sudden movement of the horse could lead to a terrible eye injury. Always be conscious of this fact, and be prepared to jerk the implement away on a half-instant's notice.
- WITHERS. The well-defined ridge between a horse's shoulder blades, where the shoulders almost meet at the top.
- WOLF TOOTH. "Extra" teeth that some horses get in front of their molars. A wolf tooth is usually sharp, and sometimes crooked as well, so that it pokes into the horse's cheek and is painful with or without a bit. Fortunately the horse seems to get immediate relief when such a tooth is pulled, and usually goes right back to normal behavior patterns.
- WORMING. "De-worming" might be a more accurate term, since when a horse is wormed, the hope is that these pushy little parasites are being removed. The battle against parasites is a constant one that you can never hope to win for long. But you can easily keep up with them, at least, by having your vet make regular checks of manure samples and then by following his instructions. *Never* use worm medicine without a vet check and his explicit instructions, as these are poisons.

Suggestions for Further Reading

No one horse book can tell you everything, so you're well advised to read all you possibly can. You'll find subjects covered in some books that are not covered in others—and you'll probably find contradictions, too. I, for instance, tell you never to feed a horse from your hand, while another author will describe in detail how to do it "properly." It's up to you to collect and compare information.

The following list of books and magazines is not complete, nor does it include fiction, which can also teach you something. But it will give you some material to get you started. For additional suggestions, try the bookstores, the libraries, and the catalogs put out by suppliers of tack and riding clothing.

GENERAL BOOKS

Coggins, Jack. *The Horseman's Bible*. Garden City, N.Y.: Doubleday, 1966.

Davidson, Joseph B. *Horsemen's Veterinary Advisor*. New York: Arco, 1974.

Hess, Lilo. *Shetland Ponies*. New York: Crowell, 1964.

Howard, Harriet Shriver. *If You Had a Pony*. New York: Harper & Row, 1965.

Hoyt, Olga. *If You Want a Horse*. New York: Coward-McCann, 1966.

Hunt, Frazier and Robert. *Horses and Heroes*. New York: Scribner's, 1949.

Ipcar, Dahlov. *Horses of Long Ago*. Garden City, N.Y.: Doubleday, 1965.

Isenbart, Hans Heinrich, and Anders, Hanns-Jorg. *A Foal Is Born*. New York: Putnam's, 1976.

Mather, Helen. *Light Horsekeeping*. New York: Dutton, 1970.

Radlauer, Ruth S. and Edward. *Horses*. Glendale, Calif.: Bowmar Pub. Corp., 1968.

Self, Margaret Cabell. *The Horseman's Encyclopedia,* rev. ed. New York: Barnes, 1963.

Slaughter, Jean. *Pony Care*. New York: Knopf, 1961.

Stull, Sally. *What You Can Do with a Horse*. South Brunswick, N.J.; Barnes, 1977.

BOOKS ON RIDING

Crabtree, Helen K. *Saddle Seat Equitation*. Garden City, N.Y.: Doubleday, 1970.

Disston, Harry. *Elementary Dressage*. South Brunswick, N.J.: Barnes, 1970.

Farshler, Earl R. *Riding and Training*, 2nd ed. Princeton, N.J.: Van Nostrand, 1959.

Holmelund, Paul. *The Art of Horsemanship*. New York: Barnes, 1962.

Hope, C. G. *The Horseman's Manual*. New York: Scribner's, 1976.

Paillard, Jean S. *Understanding Equitation*. Garden City, N.Y.: Doubleday, 1974.

Sports Illustrated. *Book of Horseback Riding.* Philadelphia: Lippincott, 1977.

Steinkraus, William. *Riding and Jumping,* rev. ed. Garden City, N.Y.: Doubleday, 1969.

Taylor, Louis. *Ride American.* New York: Harper & Row, 1963.

Van Tuyl, Barbara. *How to Ride and Jump Your Best.* New York: Grosset & Dunlap, 1973.

Wright, Gordon. *Learning to Ride, Hunt and Show.* Garden City, N.Y.: Doubleday, 1960.

MAGAZINES

American Horseman (general)

Appaloosa News

Arabian Horse News

Blood-Horse (Thoroughbreds)

Eastern-Western Quarter Horse Journal

Hoof Beats (Standardbreds)

Horse, of Course! (general)

Horse and Horseman (general)

Horse Lovers' National Magazine (general)

Horse & Rider (general)

Horse World (saddle seat show horses and ponies)

Horseman (western riding)

Horsetrader (classified ads)

National Horseman (saddle seat show horses and ponies)

Palomino Horses

Pinto Horse

Quarter Horse Journal

Saddle and Bridle (saddle seat show horses and ponies)

Western Horseman (western riding)

Index